TRIUMPHANT OVERCOMER

Presented by LaKesha L. Williams

TRIUMPHANT OVERCOMER

Copyright © 2019 by LaKesha L. Williams

All rights reserved. No part of this book may be reproduced or transmitted in any form or by any means without written permission from the author.

ISBN 978-1-7339413-7-2

Printed in USA by The Vision to Fruition Publishing House
www.vision-fruition.com

DEDICATION

To those whom God has used to help me overcome and live triumphantly; Maggie, Doris, Cleo, Rae, Anthony, Shavon, Chris, Latricia and Margo, this book is dedicated to you!

To every overcomer seeking to live triumphantly, this book is also dedicated to you!

TABLE OF CONTENTS

An Overcomers Prayer 5

Preface 7

Introduction 13

He Kept Me 27

Guilty 47

Me, My Faith and God's Favor 65

Love Don't Leave You Bruised 91

Triumphant Overcomers 109

Are You a Triumphant Overcomer? 123

An Overcomers Prayer 133

About the Visionary Author 137

About the Publisher 141

AN OVERCOMERS PRAYER

Father God, I pray for each person reading this book. I know You did not allow them to purchase or receive this book by coincidence, because everything You allow has a purpose! So, Father God, I lay them at Your feet today. I pray that the eyes of the heart of each reader may be enlightened, so they will know what the hope of Your calling is, and what the riches are of the glory of Your inheritance in the saints. May they know the surpassing greatness of Your power toward us who believe. I pray their spiritual ears will open to receive revelation as the words You have inspired in these pages. Father God meet them where they are and bring them into a greater understanding of who You are and why You allow tests and trials in our lives. I pray, in the matchless, mighty name of Jesus Christ, my Lord and Savior, Amen.

TRIUMPHANT DEFINITION
/trīˈəmfənt/

Adjective

1. having won a battle or contest; victorious.
   Synonyms: victorious, successful, winning, prize-winning, conquering
2. feeling or expressing jubilation after having won a victory or mastered a difficulty.
   Synonyms: jubilant, exultant, elated, rejoicing, joyful, joyous, delighted, gleeful, proud, cock-a-hoop; gloating, boastful, swaggering

OVERCOMER DEFINITION
\ ˌō-vər-ˈkə-mər \

Noun

1. a person who overcomes something: one who succeeds in dealing with or gaining control of some problem or difficulty
   Synonyms: defeater, subduer, surmounter, prevailer, winner

PREFACE

I am honored that you are reading this book right now. I am even more honored that you have made the choice to take this journey with us. This book is the next installment in the Born Overcomers Series. I want to take a moment to talk about how these books came about.

I was nearing my 29th birthday when I found myself thinking about my life and recalling all I've been through. As people, places, things, events, and experiences flashed through my mind I thought, "Man, that would be a pretty interesting book to read," but I had no clue how to write a book or where to start, so, I started a blog. I had a small following, but I still felt the urge to write a book, though I hadn't followed through at that time. About a year passed, and I began seeing a therapist to heal some unresolved issues. These therapy sessions helped me realize a lot about myself, all God had done in my life and all God wanted to do through my life. With the encouragement of my therapist and these discoveries, I finally began writing the book.

In the beginning, the title was *The Promise*, and I planned on guiding readers through four steps (the pain, the process, the purpose, and the promise) that would lead to discovering your purpose in life and accepting the promise and call God had for your life. I wrote one chapter and was stuck for six months. No new ideas were flowing. I was so frustrated because I knew God called me to write a book, but I couldn't figure out why I was hitting a stumbling block. I had begun sharing my testimony on Social Media, so why was it so hard to write? Little did I know God had other plans for how this book was going to come about and all that would be connected to it.

January 31, 2014, my employment status changed, from gainfully employed to unemployed. God revealed to me then that there was so much more He wanted me to do in this life than just work as a Service Desk Team Lead in Information Technology. This caused me to begin seeking Him to figure out what my next step was. Between February and May of 2014, God continuously revealed things to me and confirmed things in my spirit about how He wanted me to share my testimony and be an encouragement to His people.

One day, I was meeting with Kelley Perry, who is one of the best business coaches in the game. Although we were getting to know each other and talking about our businesses, she inspired me to finish what I'd started months ago. A fire was ignited. Later that day, I went to the library to spend some time with God, and to seek Him about His purpose for my life. On that Monday, June 2, 2014, God birthed the first book.

I was praying and asking God, "What is it that You want people to feel or take away from this book?" God revealed to me that all I've witnessed, all I've endured and all I've overcome could be used as tools to inspire, encourage and impact others. The foundation of why I share my testimony has always been Revelation 12:11 (KJV), which says, *"And they overcame him by the blood of the Lamb, and by the word of their testimony, and they loved not their lives unto the death."* From this scripture I began to search and cross-reference scriptures, searching for a different title for the book because I was no longer feeling **The Promise**.

At first, I came up with **We Shall Overcome**, but that just didn't resonate with me. I continued searching the Bible and reading the reference scriptures attached to Revelation 12:11. The next title I thought of was ***The Blood of the Lamb***, but that one did not click in my spirit either because I felt it didn't fit a book about a person's testimony. So, I continued searching and I came across Psalms 139:16 (NLT) which says, *"You saw me before I was born. Every day of my life was recorded in Your book. Every moment was laid out before a single day had passed."*

This scripture struck me, and I kept reading it repeatedly until this came to me, *"If God knew me before I was born, then He must've known all I would endure in life, which means He equipped me, and even built me to overcome everything I would experience before the foundation of the world. Therefore, I was Born to Overcome!"* With that epiphany, I discovered the title of the first book: ***Born Overcomers***!

From that moment on God began revealing things to me about the book and what He wanted me to do. He showed me **"*Born Overcomers*"** was going to be more than just a book. All of this happened on Monday, June 2, 2014, between 1:00 pm and 4:00 pm.

I was sharing how God had given me the book title with a close friend on Wednesday, June 4, 2014, and she mentioned something about a conference, and that same day I began looking for venues for the 1st Annual Born Overcomers Conference. I also developed a website and filed for incorporation with the State of Maryland for Born Overcomers Inc. By the end of the week, Born Overcomers had developed a following, I had a team on board to help me and we decided on a location to hold the first conference.

As I write this, it is now October 2019, and it has been five years, four months and 26 days since God birth Born Overcomers. I have written one book, five devotionals, co-authored an anthology with actress and comedian Kim Coles and organized two collaborations with several amazing men and women. God has allowed Born Overcomers Inc. to become a recognized non-profit organization that holds annual conferences, monthly testimony parties and provides outreach in the community.

I am grateful to God for using me to birth this ministry and this new book. I pray that you're encouraged by what you read. The purpose of this book is to encourage and inspire others to live triumphantly! Think of this book as a reminder, to get you to think differently about how you see suffering and sin, how you react to them and how you can use what you experience in life to bring fame and glory to God. After reading this book, I pray, you will have a desire to live triumphantly! I pray you will feel inspired to endure, overcome and live through life's tests and trials.

Seek God as you read this book, ask Him to reveal areas in your life where you feel like you are not living triumphantly. Search and memorize scriptures related to those areas and earnestly seek to not only overcome them but use them to live the triumphant live God predestined for you to live. Selah!

INTRODUCTION

It will lead to an opportunity for your testimony.
Luke 21:13

Psalm 22:22 says, *"I will tell of Your name to my brethren; In the midst of the assembly I will praise You."* David would praise God in the assembly because his private deliverance deserved a public testimony. God wonderfully delivers us in the quiet moments when we are hurting, and we must be prepared to offer public praise for His care.

In the pages that follow, you will read the testimonies of five amazing men and women who endured some of the hardest tests and emerged triumphantly. These triumphant overcomers are simply honoring the Lord by bearing witness to His work in their lives.

The Lord commends sharing testimonies throughout His Word, particularly in the Psalms. We continually read of the Psalmist promising to tell of the greatness of the Lord *"in the midst of the congregation."*

Often, he asks the Lord to deliver him so that he can testify of God's salvation.

The Bible is filled with the most powerful stories we will ever read or hear, but it isn't just a storybook! It is God's testimony to each of us. Now we are all part of God's story. If you have never accepted Jesus Christ as your personal Lord and Savior, you are the reason that He sent His Only Begotten Son to Calvary over 2000 years ago! If you are a believer, then you are also a part of God's story. As Christians we are to repeat the story of God's love to others who need to hear it. That includes the nations around the world, the neighbor across the street and every person like you who will read this book.

Let's stop and talk about what accepting Jesus Christ as your personal Lord and Savior looks like, and if you don't know Christ this is where you can begin a relationship with Him, right here, right now by praying the Prayer of Salvation!

CONFESSING OUR SIN

When we pray the prayer of salvation, we're admitting that we've sinned. As the Bible says of everyone, save Christ alone: "*For all have sinned, and fall short of the glory of God*" (Romans 3:23, NASB).

Some sins seem bigger than others because their obvious consequences are more serious. Murder, for example, seems to us to be worse than hatred, and adultery seems worse than lust. All sins make us sinners, and all sin cuts us off from our Holy God. All sin, therefore, leads to death because it disqualifies us from living with God, regardless of how great or small it seems. Don't minimize "little" sins or overrate "big" sins. They all separate us from God, but they all can be forgiven.

To sin is simply to fall short of the mark, like an arrow that does not quite hit the bulls-eye. The glory of God, that we fall short of is found only in Jesus Christ. Second Corinthians 4:6 (NKJV) says, "*For it is the God who commanded light to shine out of darkness, who has shone in our hearts to give the light of the knowledge of the glory of God in the face of Jesus Christ.*"

The prayer of salvation, then, recognizes that Jesus Christ is the only human who ever lived without sin. Second Corinthians 5:21 (NASB) says, "*He made Him who knew no sin to be sin on our behalf so that we might become the righteousness of God in Him."* When we trust in Christ, we make an exchange – our sin for His righteousness. Our sin was poured into Christ at His crucifixion. His righteousness is poured into us at our conversion. This is what Christians mean by Christ's atonement for sin. In the world, bartering works only when two people exchange goods of relatively equal value. But God offers to trade His righteousness for our sin – something of immeasurable worth for something completely worthless. How grateful we should be for His kindness to us.

PROFESSING FAITH IN CHRIST AS YOUR SAVIOR AND LORD

With Christ as our standard of perfection, we're now acknowledging faith in Him as God, agreeing with the Apostle John in John 1:1-3 (NASB), where it says, *"In the beginning was the Word (Christ), and the Word was with God, and the Word was God. He was in the beginning with God. All things were made through Him, and without Him, nothing was made that was made."* When God created, He made something out of nothing. Since we are created beings, we have no basis for pride. Remember that you exist only because God made you, and you have special gifts only because God gave them to you. With God you are something valuable and unique; apart from God you are nothing, and if you try to live without Him, you will be abandoning the purpose for which you were made.

God could only accept a perfect, sinless sacrifice, and since He knew that we could not possibly accomplish that, He sent His Son to die for us and pay the eternal price. "*For God so loved the world that He gave His Only Begotten Son, that whoever believes in Him should not perish but have everlasting life.*" (John 3:16, NASB)

The entire gospel of John comes to a focus in 3:16. God's love is not static or self-centered; it reaches out and draws others in. Here God sets the pattern of true love, the basis for all relationships – when you love someone dearly, you are willing to give freely to the point of self-sacrifice. God paid dearly with the life of His Son, the highest price He could pay. Jesus accepted our punishment, paid the price for our sins, and then offered us the new life that He bought for us. When we share the gospel with others, our love must be like Jesus' – willingly giving up our own comfort and security so that others might join us in receiving Gods' love.

Some people are repulsed by the idea of eternal life because their lives are miserable; but eternal life is not an extension of a person's miserable, mortal life, rather eternal life is Gods' life embodied in Christ given to all believers now as a guarantee that they will live forever. In eternal life, there is no death, sickness, enemy, evil, or sin. When we don't know Christ, we make choices as though this life is all we have. This life is just an introduction to eternity. Receive this new life by faith and begin to evaluate all that happens from an eternal perspective.

To "believe" is more than intellectual agreement that Jesus is God. It means to put our trust and confidence in Him that He alone can save us. It means to put Christ in charge of our present plans and eternal destiny. Believing is both trusting His Word as reliable and relying on Him for the power to change and overcome. If you have never trusted Christ, let this promise of everlasting life be yours today!

SAY IT ALOUD & MEAN IT NOW!

Do you agree with everything you have read so far? If you do, don't wait a moment longer to start your new life in Jesus Christ. Remember, this prayer is not a magical formula. You are simply expressing your heart to God. Pray this with me:

"Father, I know that I have broken Your laws and my sins have separated me from You. I am truly sorry, and now I want to turn away from my past sinful life, toward You. Please forgive me and help me avoid sinning again. I believe that Your Son, Jesus Christ died for my sins, was resurrected from the dead, is alive, and hears my prayer. I invite Jesus to become the Lord of my life, to rule and reign in my heart from this day forward. Please send your Holy Spirit to help me obey You, and to do Your will for the rest of my life. In Jesus' name, I pray, Amen."

I'VE PRAYED IT; NOW WHAT?

If you've prayed this prayer of salvation with true conviction and heart, you are now a follower of Jesus. This is a fact, whether you feel any different or not. Religious systems may have led you to believe that you should feel something - a warm glow, a tingle, or some other mystical feeling. The fact is, you may, or you may not. If you have prayed the prayer of salvation and meant it, you are now a follower of Jesus. The Bible tells us that your eternal salvation is secure, *"that if you confess with your mouth the Lord Jesus and believe in your heart that God has raised Him from the dead, you will be saved"* (Romans 10:9, NASB).

Welcome to the family of God! I encourage you now to find a local church where you can be baptized and grow in the knowledge of God through His Word, the Bible. Now back to our regularly schedule programming.

And the life was manifested, and we have seen and testify and proclaim to you the eternal life, which was with the Father and was manifested to us — what we have seen and heard we proclaim to you also, so that you too may have fellowship with us; and indeed our fellowship is with the Father, and with His Son Jesus Christ.
First John 1:2-3

In this passage we find that John, who walked with Jesus, was now sharing that story with his readers. He was testifying, announcing the Good News of Jesus to those who would listen.

Did you catch the word, "testify"? I grew up watching a lot of TV, crime dramas in particular. With most there is always bound to be a courtroom scene where someone is being sworn in. If I heard the swearing in of a witness once, I heard it a billion times. "Do you solemnly swear that the testimony that you are about to give is the truth and nothing but the truth, so help you God?" What does this tell us? That I watched too much TV? Yes, but it tells us something about giving a testimony. We are to tell the truth!

There is something else we need to understand about a testimony. It is about what we know to be the truth . . . not what we think or what we have heard. It is all about what we know! That's exactly what God expects from each of His followers - to simply share what we know - to testify to others of what God has done in our lives; to what we have seen Him do in our lives. We don't have to have the Bible memorized or be able to answer every question that someone might have about God. We only have to be willing to share the story of what God did in our lives!

During His time on earth that's exactly what happened. Jesus would work in someone's life and they would simply share that story with others.

In the New Testament, the Gospels and the Book of Acts provide us with many examples of men and women who testify about what Jesus has done for them. Here are a few:

When Jesus healed the blind man:

So, a second time they called the man who had been blind, and said to him, "Give glory to God; we know that this man is a sinner." He then answered, "Whether He is a sinner, I do not know; one thing I do know, that though I was blind, now I see."
John 9:24-25

By now the man who was blind had heard the same questions over and over by the Pharisees. He did not know how or why he was healed, but he knew that his life had been miraculously changed, and he was not afraid to tell the truth. You don't need to know all the answers in order to share Christ with others. It is important to tell how He has changed your life. Then trust that God will use your words to help others believe in Him too!

When Jesus forgave the Samaritan woman:

Come, see a man who told me all the things that I have done; this is not the Christ, is it?
John 4:29

And they were saying to the woman, "It is no longer because of what you said that we believe, for we have heard for ourselves and know that this One is indeed the Savior of the world."
John 4:42

The disciples were simply ordinary men who told people the extraordinary story of Jesus working in their lives. That was what Jesus wanted them to do, it's what He wants us to do and it's what you will find in the pages that follow!

And you will testify also, because you have been with Me from the beginning.
John 15:27

The saints in Revelation 12:10-11 are said to have overcome Satan *"by the blood of the Lamb and by the word of their testimony."* Whatever the exact nature of this testimony, we know they were publicly identifying with Jesus Christ despite the opposition of Satan.

A principle emerges across the pages of Scripture: one of God's design in saving us is that we will, in turn, honor Him by sharing our testimony with others.

The world needs Christians who will not be afraid to live their faith and share their testimony. The Lord commanded us to go into all the world and preach the gospel. We will not be able to do that unless we realize the power and importance of our testimony.

Come and hear, all who fear God, and I will tell of what He has done for my soul.
Psalm 66:16

Our prayer is that, in the testimonies on the pages that follow, you will be inspired and encouraged not just to overcome your current tests and trials but to have the courage to share with others what the Lord has done for you, that is how we live as triumphant overcomers.

Lisa Council
HE KEPT ME

DAMAGED LENS

She-is-Me. My words & thoughts shape & mold her; My actions affect her both positively and negatively; All that I do has influence and power to balm or harm her!!!

Who is she? No one seems to know...not even her. She was small in stature, dark chocolate covered skin, and long thick ponytails that trickled down her back and cascaded in the wind. Her smile was so charming and all too cute...yet seemingly sad. There was one deep perfect round dimple planted on her right cheek and her dark brown bubbly eyes were Barbie doll bright, weary and unique. Her mom would always dress her like a little royal princess from head to toe, nothing was ever out of order, and every stitch of her clothing had its own magical flow. Bright colors stood out in her mind, especially yellow most of the time, she was often dressed in the exact same details as her older sibling; her sisters signature color was pink and hers was blue...not one of her favorite colors, but mom

He Kept Me

didn't have a clue. How could the little chocolate drop detest herself so much? Is it even possible for a child to know what hate is? Isn't the life of a child supposed to be happy go lucky and carefree? She remembers hearing those adult observations when it came to her; her looks, her character and her traits...she's bad, she's ugly, she's cute to be so dark, how did she get such long flowing locks? She's fast, she's slow, she ain't nothing but a little hoe! She'll never amount to anything and will probably end up with a lack of education and tons of kids. She would often day dream and even lay awake at night, wondering if all those things were true, how could anyone define her as such? Of course, it had to be true, because little girls don't know anything, except for what they're taught, even by not so nice adults who often times leave innocent little kids living in a rut. Sadly, this became little chocolate drops normal description and her way of perceiving, surveying and listening, so she accepted, believed and embraced it. She was indeed the bad seed, everything that she did even if it was right, it was still wrong. All the dreams that she had were shattered. Those dreams of becoming the next Diana Ross, a super model, a millionaire, well-educated and holding down her own…none of that mattered. Life as she knew it turned into a world-wind of hell, low esteem, abusive relationships, self-destruction, and a bad temper full of rage landed her in a jail cell. Could there possibly be another way of life, as little chocolate drop turned big chocolate drop, she had to try something different, she wanted so desperately to put an end to a life of misery. It had to STOP!! A misery that wasn't even caused by her, yet that was an unfolding mystery. Could it have been that all this time, she was viewing herself through someone else's sight, someone who had no way of seeing clearly past their own dimmed light.

All too often we see ourselves as others see us. We must not view ourselves through the eyes, feelings and words of man. It is imperative that we see ourselves the way that God see's us, as God created us in His image.

Scripture:
So, God created man in His own image, in the image of God He created him; male and female He created them.
Genesis 1:27 (KJV)

He Kept Me

For I consider that the sufferings of this present time are not worthy to be compared with the glory which shall be revealed in us.

Romans 8:18 (KJV)

Action:

- Surrender your pain to God and ask for healing.
- Be intentional about practicing self-love and self-respect.
- Create and find things that bring you joy.

BLURRED SIGHT

My lavish cocoon of self-doubt, pity parties, bitterness, hatred, anger and resentment was becoming uncomfortable. I desperately desired something different, wider, higher, brighter…I desired peace. I was slowly and reluctantly coming to terms that no matter how painful or uncomfortable the process of change might be; it was imperative for me to face, be open to admit and accept my past. I could no longer hold on to unresolved hurt, trauma and pain. This meant admitting my own guilt as well, which is in fact simply and sadly this…During my many years of being in abusive relationships, there were countless times that I cried out to God to end it and if He did, it would be my last...that was a BIG LIE!!! I would often cry out that I didn't deserve to be abused, cheated on, mistreated; but the truth of the matter is this...I only wanted "out" for that moment. I stayed in unhealthy long-term committed relationships including holy (unholy) matrimony for various reasons; money, sex, quality and comfort to a certain lifestyle, fear of change, co-dependency, bonds and connections with family and friends, low self-esteem, shame, embarrassment and last but not least...pride. The painful confession is that...self-inflicted Russian roulette was my game of choice, it had become my very own high-end sport!!! I had to come to the realization that suppressed feelings equal danger! I had to set the record straight for my own well-being, wholeness and sake; as long as I was walking around with unresolved issues, sucking up my feelings, convincing myself that the pain would somehow magically disappear, sweeping deadly secrets and emotions under the rug and not seeking the proper help that was needed heal and move forward, I would continue to be a walking time bomb; merely living to cope. Somedays I tried to convince myself that it would be easier to turn to a life

He Kept Me

of dope; but there was a still firm voice that would always yell NOPE!!! While the journey of becoming was quite a challenge, I had to move forward to discover a healthy balance. There were days when it was so much easier to go back to being that person that I never wanted to be, the unhealthy relationships, fake and phony friendships, the lies of me trying to convince myself that I just wasn't good enough, the voices in head trying to turn back to my past and just give up. Funny thing about it all, is that somewhere in the back of my mind, I knew that I was beautiful, special and unique; yet I was depleted of self-love and my soul was weak. The thought of moving forward was truly debilitating for me, although I desired to grow, and thrive, I had to work hard through my pain to in order survive. I had to accept the fact that in order to be free, I had to let go of the thoughts, the people and all the things that weren't meant to be. I had to accept the fact that I couldn't pack my heavy, old and rusty baggage in my newly shined light colorful luggage. As I was still fighting hard to hold on, anything that was no longer aligned with my fight for healing, freedom and life would be removed.

Lisa Council

The process of becoming me; the me that God called me to be was feeling love, peace and victory. The little turned big chocolate drop was finally in a place of flying FREE!!!

I have learned that one of the key principles to overcoming pain and thriving is to clean out our emotional closets, while we always hear the saying "just let go or get over it" we must come to terms with the fact that the pain, trauma, disappointments, and setbacks that we've endured in life aren't going anywhere until we decide to do our part in releasing it.

<u>Scripture:</u>

So, if the Son sets you free, you will be free indeed.
John 8:36 (NIV)

Behold, I will do a new thing, now it shall spring forth; Shall you not know it? I will even make a road in the wilderness and rivers in the desert.
Isaiah 43:19 (NKJV)

<u>Action:</u>
- Seek profession help and or/support group.

- Surround yourself with overcomers that will inspire you and hold you accountable.
- Don't give up...stay the course.

LUMINOUS LIGHT

While looking in the mirror one morning, I asked myself the following question...why does this keep happening to me? My response...as long as you continue to supply your pain with a "full" tank of the benefit of the doubt, it will continue to leave you on "empty." I later discovered that the profound response didn't come from me, it came from God. As God continues to mold me into the person that He's called me to be, I've learned that life isn't at all as I'd desired it to be...a Cinderella Fairytale with shimmering glass slippers that fit, minus adversity.

Although I am still overcoming the trauma of seeing myself through others eyes, being raped at the age of 13, then molested by a close adult family friend in my late teens, having two failed marriages the 1st due to verbal, emotional and physical abuse and the 2nd due to the strongholds of drug and alcohol addiction, having a beautiful, bright, intelligent and loving child out of wedlock and yet another failed relationship, I can truly say that I know that it was only God that kept me!!! Even during the countless times that I wanted to give up and throw in the towel...**GOD KEPT ME**!!! When I tried to overdose on prescription meds...**GOD KEPT ME**!!! When I tried to overdose by alcohol poisoning and 50 over the counter pain relievers...**GOD KEPT ME**!!! When I drove to the bridge and tried to convince myself to jump off...**GOD KEPT ME**!!! The times when I've gotten it wrong and professed to myself that I was a horrible parent and the only way for my child to have a fair chance was to permanently remove myself from her life through taking my own...**GOD KEPT ME**!!! When I've cried non-stop and the voices in my head made me want to pop...**GOD KEPT ME**!!! When the drums from the anxiety attacks were playing over and over in my head...**GOD KEPT ME**!!! When I felt as though I was going to pass out from the uncontrollable cries and sobs, while trying to keep a fake smile for my phony mob...**GOD KEPT ME**!!! When I was singing my own lyrics of self-pity and doubt...**GOD KEPT ME**!!! When I was filled self-hate, no love and 100% of doubt...**GOD KEPT ME**!!! When I held that loaded gun to my head, dropped it and when it

He Kept Me

off, I almost shot off my left foot instead...**GOD KEPT ME!!!** When my abuser knocked me down that flight of stairs and I landed on back and not my head...**GOD KEPT ME!!!** When he tried to drown me in that tub, chocking the wind out of me, but I regained consciousness and laid for hours in a fatal position on the bathroom rug...**GOD KEPT ME!!!** When I had to sleep under the bed because I didn't know if the drug man was going to put a bullet in me and my child's head...**GOD KEPT ME!!!** When I had to miss multiple days from work because my car was stolen, returned with no gas and had been crashed...**GOD KEPT ME!!!** When the bank account was overdrawn, and he said he'd be right back and I'm looking out the window with no return in sight...**GOD KEPT ME!!!** When the migraines from stress caused uncontrollable vomiting, chills and paralyzing pain...**GOD KEPT ME!!!** When I didn't know what to expect when I put the key in the door, would my family ever see me and my child anymore...**GOD KEPT ME!!!** When the neighbor said he owes me a debt and you better pay...can I work out a payment plan Mr. Drug man; well just because I know where you and your child live, of course you can...**GOD KEPT ME!!!** Who's this stranger lurking by my windows and door...**GOD KEPT ME**!!! When I returned home, and the house was cleaned out; no breathe left in my lungs to even shout...**GOD KEPT ME**!!! When they told me, the only sister took those four bullets to her head, more than 34 stabs wounds and crushed skull...**GOD KEPT ME**!!! When my oldest brother couldn't handle it and took it all...**GOD KEPT ME**!!! When they sent my last remaining sibling home for a short, bitter, sad reunion to die...**GOD KEPT ME**!!! When I felt like this is it, I've had enough with tears streaming down my face; I ain't gonna lie...**GOD KEPT ME**!!!

As I now look back over my life, I thank God for it all!!! Though there are quite a few things that I will never understand, yet, I can rest in hope, faith and assurance that God is, has been and will always be with me, nor will He ever forsake me.

Even during my darkest times, I always wanted nothing more than to witness others shine. I would pour my heart and soul into helping others, yet when it came to me, I had no desire, to be happy, shine or fly free. Now through God's grace and mercy I am fully capable of sharing my testimony with others and

He Kept Me

insuring them that they too came and will triumphantly overcome. It is my desire to show others through my testimony that there is indeed beauty in healing. Often, we can become stagnant in the process of healing because we do not want to go through reliving the pain, I too am guilty of that. However, I am here to fully assure you that there is absolutely nothing more painful than staying stuck in a place that God so desperately wants and desires to move you from. I never imaged having a life filled with joy, peace and living on and with purpose.

In sharing my testimony, I am reminded of the story that stands out the most for me... the story Tamar, daughter of King David:

In the course of time, Amnon son of David fell in love with Tamar, the beautiful sister of Absalom son of David. ²Amnon became so obsessed with his sister Tamar that he made himself ill. She was a virgin, and it seemed impossible for him to do anything to her. ³Now Amnon had an adviser named Jonadab son of Shimeah, David's brother. Jonadab was a very shrewd man. ⁴He asked Amnon, "Why do you, the king's son, look so haggard morning after morning?

Lisa Council

Won't you tell me?" Amnon said to him, "I'm in love with Tamar, my brother Absalom's sister." ⁵"Go to bed and pretend to be ill," Jonadab said. "When your father comes to see you, say to him, 'I would like my sister Tamar to come and give me something to eat. Let her prepare the food in my sight so I may watch her and then eat it from her hand.'" ⁶So Amnon lay down and pretended to be ill. When the king came to see him, Amnon said to him, "I would like my sister Tamar to come and make some special bread in my sight, so I may eat from her hand." ⁷David sent word to Tamar at the palace: "Go to the house of your brother Amnon and prepare some food for him." ⁸So Tamar went to the house of her brother Amnon, who was lying down. She took some dough, kneaded it, made the bread in his sight and baked it. ⁹Then she took the pan and served him the bread, but he refused to eat. "Send everyone out of here," Amnon said. So, everyone left him. ¹⁰Then Amnon said to Tamar, "Bring the food here into my bedroom so I may eat from your hand." And Tamar took the bread she had prepared and brought it to her brother Amnon in his bedroom. ¹¹But when she took it to him to eat, he grabbed her and said, "Come to bed with me, my sister." ¹²"No, my brother!" she said to him. "Don't force me! Such a thing should not be done in Israel! Don't do

He Kept Me

this wicked thing. ¹³What about me? Where could I get rid of my disgrace? And what about you? You would be like one of the wicked fools in Israel. Please speak to the king; he will not keep me from being married to you." ¹⁴But he refused to listen to her, and since he was stronger than she, he raped her. ¹⁵Then Amnon hated her with intense hatred. In fact, he hated her more than he had loved her. Amnon said to her, "Get up and get out!" ¹⁶"No!" she said to him. "Sending me away would be a greater wrong than what you have already done to me." But he refused to listen to her. ¹⁷He called his personal servant and said, "Get this woman out of my sight and bolt the door after her." ¹⁸So his servant put her out and bolted the door after her. She was wearing an ornate robe, for this was the kind of garment the virgin daughters of the king wore. ¹⁹Tamar put ashes on her head and tore the ornate robe she was wearing. She put her hands on her head and went away, weeping aloud as she went. ²⁰Her brother Absalom said to her, "Has that Amnon, your brother, been with you? Be quiet for now, my sister; he is your brother. Don't take this thing to heart." And Tamar lived in her brother Absalom's house, a desolate woman.

2 Samuel 13:1-20 (NIV)

Lisa Council

I have embraced crawling through the dirt and quick sand, because I know that I'm coming out professing…YES, I CAN!!! Today I can thank God for the trials and tribulations in my life, as I now know that it was Him who carried me through. The trauma, abuse, tragedy and pain that I endured may have killed someone else, but as for me, through God's grace, it shaped and molded me to live my life triumphantly. I can now clearly see…see that I am free to be me! All the guilt, shame and blame no longer leaves me living a life of bondage and feeling like I'm entangled in chains. Through intentional transformation and healing, I am now able to teach my only child to live free from seeing through others eyes, to live life to the fullest and to continuously thrive, to live a life of love for oneself and others, as there are so many in the world that don't know where to turn and sadly their vision is often contaminated and blurred by mothers, fathers, sisters and brothers.

We all have a testimony in us, some of us have lived and experienced the strongholds of tragedy, trauma, abuse, rape, deceit, molestation, drug addiction, alcoholism, failed marriages, relationships,

He Kept Me

friendships, misfortune, abandonment, anxiety, depression, thoughts of not being good enough, and a life of unfortunate circumstances not to be shared. I am here to assure you that if you would just hold on to God's unchanging hand, sincerely cry out and lay your brokenness before Him; He will supply your healing, make you whole and grant you indescribable peace.

God does not bring us out of our wilderness to live a desolate life, Him wants us to live freely, as victorious overcomers, strong, mighty and triumphant!!!

Scripture:

God is in the midst of her, she shall not be moved.
Psalm 46:5 (NKJV)

Strength and honor are her clothing; She shall rejoice in time to come.
Proverbs 31:25 (NKJV)

Action:

- Continue to invite God in.

Lisa Council

- Stay in God's word and strive to walk in obedience.
- Share your testimony with others. There are others who need your story so that they too, may be set free.

He Kept Me

Lisa Council

Lisa Council is a survivor of domestic violence who shares her testimony of overcoming abuse and tragedy. Her story is shared in schools, churches and conferences. Lisa is a co-author in the International Amazon Bestseller ***Restoration Speaks Loud: From Tragedy to Triumph*** and Amazon Bestseller ***I Am Her Story – From Pain to Purpose I: Testimonies of Strong Women***.

Lisa's story *I Am Lynda's Voice* has aired on DCTV and was featured in the 2017 DC Black Film Festival, winning 1st place in the category of "Best Web Series."

Lisa Council

She has also been featured in the Purple Pearls Magazine *I Overcame Project* and Federal City Alumnae Chapter of Delta Sigma Theta Sorority, Inc.'s *My Sister's Keeper: Addressing Violence Against Women and Children*.

Lisa's greatest passion is empowering women and young girls, assuring them that they too can live a life free of bondage and be healed from all adversity and to see themselves as God sees them...royalty. [1 Peter 2:9]

Lisa is the daughter to Mr. and Mrs. James Fleet and the late Walter Council. Lisa is a proud mother and a native Washingtonian.

Lisa knows that *"it was in her darkness that God was preparing her for her destiny!"* [Psalm 46:5]

Contact
Email: dixon.lisa14@yahoo.com
Phone: (202) 330-1125
Facebook: Lisa Council

He Kept Me
Acknowledgements

First, I would like to thank My Lord and Savior Jesus Christ

My Daughter, T'Maya Simmons

My Parents, James and Beverly Fleet

My Pastor Damon Parran, First Lady Tamika and my EChurch Family

Also, I would like to acknowledge my family and loved ones and The Vision to Fruition Publishing House.

Kenneth Baldwin

GUILTY

I'm GUILTY of all this work I have done, and you are going to deny me??? That is me speaking to the Department of Health and Professional Licensing Board Committee.

Rewind…it was the summer of July 2009; I went to the licensing board to submit my application for consideration for eligibility of becoming a Certified Addictions Counselor. I was informed that I was too late; the laws had changed and you now must have at least an Associate's degree to qualify for consideration. I had recently completed a Counseling Education program provided through Catholic Charities in December 2008. I procrastinated…I was GUILTY of submitting my application past the deadline, after the criteria changed, and it fell into the pool of candidates who had to provide college credits and degrees to prove worthiness.

I was employed as well as mentoring adjudicated youth at the time. I was also facilitating a critical thinking group to sanctioned offenders in my city.

Guilty

These two activities gave me a sense of purpose. I was transitioning from drugging and incarceration to a place where I felt I was making a difference in my community.

It would be three more years before I ventured to meet the requirements to apply for the Certified Addictions Counselor Certification again. In the interim, in 2010, I was found GUILTY, at least in the judge's eyesight, of simple assault (domestic). I had to participate in a twenty-two-week course for domestic violence (DV). I learned a lot of information during that program. The information propelled me to seek further education. I attended a training in Athens, Tennessee and obtained a certification for Creating a Process of Change for Men who Batter, a Duluth Model training. I stayed on at the DV twenty-two-week course group for another two years as a peer facilitator.

In 2011, I was charged with carrying a pistol without a license. Being a convicted felon, I still had a motto "It is better to have it and not it, than to need it and not have it." Upon reflection, I was GUILTY of holding on to a mindset that served me well in one culture but not necessarily in a societal norm. It was a turning point. Although I had the mindset to carry a firearm; I still was mentoring adjudicated youth. It was my effort to decrease the vicious cycle of self-hatred, indoctrination of slave mentality, and basic animalistic living in our future generations.

I recall an incident going to the Department of Youth Rehabilitation Services (DYRS), I was hassled about my entrance to see one of my youths. The hassle stemmed from me having an ankle bracelet on tracking my movements in the community. The staff felt it was an incongruency for me to be mentoring with a device strapped to my leg. I was in agreement that the monitor needed to come off, as to not hinder my progress I was experiencing with youth finding their way on the journey of life.

I voiced my concerns with a colleague, and my attorney I secured for the gun offense. I was able to get a hearing with the judge requesting the removal of the ankle monitor. The prosecutor reminded the judge that I had a lengthy record and had concerns about removing the device.

Guilty

The judge acknowledged the prosecutor concerns and gave his thoughts to the court for the record. The judge agreed with the prosecutor about my history with the criminal justice system. He also informed the prosecutor that looking at the record of the court regarding Mr. Baldwin, he would be reluctant to grant my motion but "That is not the man standing before you. This paper does not accurately reflect the totality of who Mr. Baldwin is at present. In light of this information, I am granting Mr. Baldwin's motion for removal of the GPS (global positioning system) from his ankle." My mentoring with the youth being detained at DYRS continued without incident.

I was able overcome that charge after filing a motion for suppression of evidence. My lawyer was able to suppress the evidence of the firearm on the grounds that it was an illegal search by the police. Even after having the motion granted, my PO still thought I was GUILTY. When I presented her with the case dismissed papers, she asked, "How did you beat this case." It was favor.

Kenneth Baldwin

In 2012, I finally made the decision to enroll in school (Catholic University) to receive my Associate's through a partnership from Catholic Charities Counseling Education Program. Upon receiving my Associate degree, I qualified to apply for the Addictions Counselor certification.

I had been mentoring and facilitating critical thinking groups for about four years. I had a desire to secure contracts with the government to facilitate in other arenas, as well as the criminal justice population. A friend indicated that "You are not going to get far with the contracts without some paperwork behind you."

There was some resistance from certain individuals who realized I was having an impact on participants. The impact came from lived experience. That upset the people from academia who did not want to validate the connection being made between the clients and myself. This fueled the desire to return to school. Complementing my practical experience with a theoretical base would solidify my qualifications to present to this population.

Guilty

It would actually be twenty-nine years, from my high school graduation before I attained a college degree. Thirty-one years to receive my bachelor's degree. Once I began the process, I broadened my vision to go the entire limit. Mind you, I only had to present an Associate degree to be eligible to sit for the certification test. Returning to school renewed a thirst for a knowledge base to support myself and empower others.

It has been a struggle at times, due to the fact that, I maintained full time employment my entire academic journey; along with a full load schedule. Despite the challenge, I graduated Cum Laude and was awarded the UPCEA Outstanding Continuing Education Student Award. I was nominated by the University. It was the school's first time ever nominating a student. The nomination for the Mid-Atlantic Region is for students from District of Columbia, Delaware, Maryland, New Jersey, New York, Pennsylvania, and Ontario, Canada. That award was a great honor that impacted me to continue pursuing academic excellence.

Kenneth Baldwin

The dilemma. I submitted my paperwork for consideration and was rejected. The reasons for my rejection was me being GUILTY.

Dear Mr. Baldwin:

On December 8, 2015, you submitted an application to be certified as an addiction counselor. After reviewing your application, the Board has decided to ask you to withdraw it. The Board cites as its reasoning for the request, your numerous convictions between the years of 1992 and 2003 – five felonies and twelve misdemeanors.

D.C. Official Code § 3-1205.14(a)(4)(C) authorizes the Board of Professional Counseling to deny an application for certification for someone who has been convicted of a crime of "moral turpitude." The Code defines "moral turpitude" as a crime that: (A) Offends the generally accepted moral code of mankind; (B) Is one of baseness, vileness, or depravity in the conduct of the private and social duties that an individual owes to his or her fellow man or to society in general; or (C) Is one of conduct contrary to justice, honesty, modesty, or good morals.

The Board is of the opinion that the crimes for which you were convicted fall within the definition of "moral turpitude." The decision to withdraw your application is entirely up to you. If you choose not to withdraw, the Board will request the Office of the Attorney General to prepare a "Notice of Intent to Deny" [certification]. After you are served the "Notice" you will be entitled to all due process rights as provided by District law.

Signed,

During my holding pattern, awaiting my court date I secured several recommendations to advance my application. In addition, it was a reflection period to self-examine my life. A time to review all the events that had led me to this juncture.

In retrospect, I was GUILTY. GUILTY of crimes I cannot speak of. GUILTY of several abuses. I have committed physical abuse, verbal abuse, and substance abuse. The physical abuse was two-fold. I was a victim of abuse by those who were considered friends. I, in turn

Guilty

became a perpetrator of physical abuse to those who considered me a friend and towards some strangers. I verbally abused those I'd been in relationships with and people who thought that they were wittier or craftier than me. I abused substances for better than two decades. Drugs were the motivating factor for ninety percent of my arrests.

I had been labeled a menace to society due to my many arrests and convictions. I was GUILTY for taking from a host of entities. I took from my community (GUILTY). At several of my arrests the community applauded. They were able to find relief in the fact that I was removed from society for a period of time. Store owners, homeowners, businesses and the like had been victims of my insane wayward and reckless behavior. I took peace from my family (GUILTY). That behavior had affected my family deeply. They could not fathom what went wrong for me to behave so far removed from the values that they instilled in me. Their peace was taken having to wonder daily if they were going to receive a call to identify my body. Plenty of prayers were lifted by family to protect me in the wilderness of the concrete jungle.

Kenneth Baldwin

My mother instilled a lot of great values in me. She taught me to be tactful, concede to minute issues taking the high road. She taught me to display good manners, respect your elders and have compassion. At the time, I felt she was imparting tools to be weak. That was felt because as I deviated from the nest and ark of safety, those individuals I surrounded myself with were not displaying those attributes. I am not saying that they did not have similar values. I am saying no one was displaying them on the corners and in the school yards.

I always had manners. My grandmother would always say "Manners will take you places that money can't." I utilized that tool to get access to a lot of people. I never forgot that message. In the wild, straddling the fence could have grave consequences. I began to diminish the concepts I knew to be right and acquire another set of concepts that helped me adjust to the jungle of criminality and addiction.

In adopting those other ideologies, I took peace from myself; inner peace (GUILTY). Mental agony was a crushing weight on me constantly. Knowing I was living in direct opposition to my upbringing and

Guilty

training brought about a lot of self-condemnation and grief. These tribulations have plagued me for years.

> [11] *If by any means I might attain unto the resurrection of the dead.* [12] *Not as though I had already attained, either were already perfect: but I follow after, if that I may apprehend that for which also, I am apprehended of Christ Jesus.* [13] *Brethren, I count not myself to have apprehended: but this one thing I do, forgetting those things which are behind, and reaching forth unto those things which are before,* [14] *I press toward the mark for the prize of the high calling of God in Christ Jesus.*
> Philippians 3:11-14 (KJV)

Throughout this reflection, I realized although I was GUILTY of multiple offenses; I was also guilty of being a conqueror. I say conqueror because I climbed multiple mountains. Mountains of guilt, mountains of rejection, mountains of shame, mountains of powerlessness, mountains of enslavement and mountains of failure. Do you think mountain climbing is a strenuous activity? I pose this because mountain climbing was a strenuous activity for me.

Kenneth Baldwin

With regard to GUILT, I carried the guilt of being the cause of my parents failed marriage. I failed to obey a command my mother gave me which created an argument between my mother and father. Shortly, thereafter my father left us. I blamed myself for him leaving. It had nothing to do with me.

My first acknowledgement of rejection was by a young lady at a swimming pool. A young lady I had an interest in, one of whom rebuffed my advances. It hurt me, forming an image of me that said I wasn't enough. Today I use rejection as motivation and a sense of protection. I wrestled with mountains of shame, from sexual molestation, which led to multiple conquests to satisfy a mental need. I was a victim of powerlessness from witnessing domestic violence in the home. Powerlessness because I did not prevent it. My answer to preventing it was to take a life. My fear of being reported to the authorities by my mom halted that action. The dysfunction, helplessness, distortion, and suppression ultimately led me to reenact those exact same behaviors in my own home. A tumultuous road of enslavement. A slave to substances, a slave to outside validation, a slave to distorted thinking. It was

Guilty

at the height of my insanity that I conquered my mountain of failure.

This insanity gripped me with a shackle of brokenness. I was at the bottom of fifteen feet of water, drowning, waiting for the lifeguard to come down and rescue me. The lifeguard was me changing my perspective and philosophy of life. After all doors were closed, something had to give.

²And be not conformed to this world: but be ye transformed by the renewing of your mind, that ye may prove what is that good, and acceptable, and perfect, will of God.
Romans 12:2 (KJV)

In climbing those mountains and reaching those peaks, was a tremendous feeling. A wonderful feeling of triumph. While basking in that triumph, it ignited a spark to prevent others from having to experience those struggles that I endured. I desired to transfer my experiences to halt trauma and pain in others' lives. Thus, began my journey of mentoring, speaking, group facilitation, and engaging anyone who wanted to find solutions to their situations.

Kenneth Baldwin

I shared my story to foster hope in someone who may not see a way out. Someone who may have allowed doubt to consume them and kill dreams they are capable of achieving. Someone who believes they are not worthy. Not knowing that exactly where they are at present.... they are enough.

I have earned two degrees, approaching my third, along with doctoral aspirations. I am a mentor, a speaker, an overcomer, and I am a conqueror! To be quite frank, the one thing that I am now GUILTY of...I'm GUILTY of being passionate of giving back to those who see no way out and feel as though they are left behind.

Come now, and let us reason together, saith the LORD: though your sins be as scarlet, they shall be as white as snow; though they be red like crimson, they shall be as wool.
Isaiah 1:18 (KJV)

My date in front of the Board. I came prepared to present my case and illustrate why I was qualified to be given the opportunity to take the test for certification. The hearing lasted about an hour. I was

Guilty

sent to an outer room to await their decision. Their decision was in the affirmative for me. I was told if I could pass the test, I will be awarded the certification. I successfully became a Certified Addictions Counselor.

An ironic thing happened after the hearing. The liaison informed that the first day I came to contest the removal of my application; the Board had made a decision to allow me to take the test. She informed me that she could not reveal that information to me because I had lawyered up and all communication was being funneled through my attorney.

I rushed to obtain an attorney, having some fear that alone I might not prevail (GUILTY). Favor has been upon me for a long time. My haste was fueled for my desire to help those individuals who experience despair, pain, and anguish. Wanting people to operate at their highest possibility is one of my strongest desires. To motivate, empower, and inspire is my passion. Yep, help put people in a position to win. Some may see that as a weakness, some see it as a strength. For that mission to serve I AM GUILTY!

Kenneth Baldwin

Kenneth Baldwin

Kenneth Baldwin, BA, CAC is CEO and Founder of Discovery Consultants. Achieving his degree in Social Science, coupled with personal experience overcoming challenges and trauma, Mr. Baldwin has used these resources to provide education, support and guidance to victims and perpetrators of domestic violence, people who suffer from distorted thinking, and experience hopelessness.

Mr. Baldwin founded Discovery Consultants in 2008, which targets the criminal justice, substance abuse,

Guilty

and at-risk youth populations. Mr. Baldwin expanded his scope of interventions by acquiring the Domestic Abuse Intervention Program (DAIP) Duluth Model Training in 2010. While serving in these capacities, facilitating groups for the Court Services and Offender Supervision Agency (CSOSA), Mr. Baldwin has been presented with various awards and recognition for his service, including the White House Presidential Drum Major for Service Award in 2013, the Mentor of the Year Award through CSOSA Faith Based Initiative, the White House Presidential Unsung Hero Award for his volunteer efforts in 2014, and White House President's Volunteer Service Award with CSOSA-February 2016. Mr. Baldwin's training in Addictions Counseling; Domestic Violence, Anger Management, Crisis Intervention, Mentoring, and Life experience has equipped him with tools necessary to empower individuals to make transformative steps to improve their quality of life.

Mr. Baldwin also coaches individuals who desire life transformation through an independent results-oriented transformation company in Washington, DC.

Kenneth Baldwin

Contact

Email: kennethbaldwindc@yahoo.com

Phone: 202-425-8101

Facebook: Kenneth Baldwin

LinkedIn: Kenneth Baldwin

Guilty

Carol Wright
ME, MY FAITH AND GOD'S FAVOR

I wasn't born alone, three minutes after my birth, the doctor's saw another baby. To my Mom and Dad's surprise, it was my twin sister Carolyn. We weighed three pounds each and stayed in the hospital for months. We came home to meet our big brother Winnie who was nine months older than us. Nine months later my youngest brother Kirk was born.

My niece ordered me a T-shirt that reads: "Strong, Brave, Fierce", that's the way I felt about my Mom; Annie Holmes Nelson, and my Dad, James Henry Nelson, Sr. who served in the U. S. Army. Four babies in diapers at the same time, having us all in twenty-seven months.

I grew up in a small rural area called Ruther Glen, thirty miles outside of Richmond, Virginia.

My Mom was what we now call "a stay at home Mom." After my Dad returned from serving our country, he worked night shift at McGuire Hospital in Richmond, VA. My Dad was always a strong provider.

Me, My Faith and God's Favor

Me, I am like my Dad. I learned from his work ethics; he got up at 10 p.m. to drive to Richmond; he worked the midnight shift.

My brothers, and my sister and I, dominated the sports teams at Ladysmith High School. We were active in basketball, track and softball. Especially softball, I hung up my cleats when I turned 50 years old. My brother Winnie, who was named after my Dad, James Wendell Nelson, Jr. was playing basketball when he collapsed on the court and died at 32 years old. I imagine one of the hardest things for a mother to do is bury her child. My Dad died several years earlier.

In August 2007, I was baptized at my cousin Tommy's church. He is like a third brother to me. He is seven months younger than Carolyn and me and two months older than my brother Kirk. When Kirk and his family weren't living life to the fullest in Richmond, once or twice a year they are vacationing somewhere exciting. Tommy, his sisters Loretta and Zelda, my sister and I; along with my brothers were all raised up together. We are double first cousins, in case you don't know what that is, let me tell you. My mother and their father were sister and brother; and my father and their mother were sister and brother. The seven of us were always together, playing in the dirt, playing baseball with no glove, riding bikes, playing outside all day on Saturdays and walking two miles to church on Sunday. Those were the good ole days! Tommy, now Bishop Holmes, preached in his sermon recently that we were poor, but we didn't know it. We had a good life, with loving parents. I'm so blessed and so is our family, if you're ever passing through Ruther Glen on a Sunday morning, please visit our church, New Life Pentecostal Church on Jericho Road.

God started preparing me for retirement in 2016, so I thought? In reality, He was preparing to reveal I had cancer in my body. My finances were in order and I was on a strict budget for the first time, thanks to XNE Financial Advising, LLC. In 2017 I was debt free, life was good! I could move on to the next stage in my life...

STAGE 1

Imagine going to the OB GYN for your yearly pap smear? You get undressed, put on that open in the front, hospital grown while you sit there and WAIT for the doctor...

I was feeling fantastic, healthy, and blessed! In July I had a wonderful vacation in Jamaica with my sweetie! The ocean view cottage looked out at the beautiful turquoise blue waters. We walked right out to the beach in just a few steps. A few days after I returned from Jamaica my best friend Bertha called. She asked, "Are you ready to retire and travel?" My plan was to work for 5 more years then retire. She said, "I need a roommate for a 10-day Hawaii vacation!" Bertha is my best, oldest and longest friend. Thirty-nine years we've been friends! I quickly rearranged my budget, called her and said: "Yes, I'm in." The perfect cruise to continue my yearlong birthday celebration. We met in Honolulu on November 11th. We stayed in Waikiki and toured the island for 2 days. The next 7 days we cruised the islands of Hawaii, unbelievably breathtaking! The most beautiful God-made scenery I had ever seen! We cruised to the islands of Maui, Hilo, Kona and Kauai. Delicious food is what we ate at the exclusive restaurants on board the ship, where you had to reserve tables in advance. This was my first time staying in a suite! Georgia, our personal assistant, took extraordinary care of us, she even surprised me with birthday decorations and a party! What a year of fun, relaxing, and exciting trips.

December 12th was just another day as I waited for my doctor. I looked at the pictures from vacation and laughed. When she arrived, we chatted for a couple of minutes about my Jamaica and Hawaii trips. I laid back on the table, knees bent, feet up in the stirrups as she did her exams. After she did the pap, I raised my arms above my head; and she examined my breast. Nothing different, she's been my doctor for 10 years. I was getting dressed, and she said, "We've talked about your breast before," I said, "Yes they've always been inverted," and smiled. I had just done my yearly mammogram four months ago in August. When she said, "I want you to see a breast surgeon," I thought it was a part of getting older; she probably recommended this for all women my age. On November 23, I turned 60 years old. I don't look my age, I eat healthy foods, and I felt great weighing in at 120 pounds! I didn't think twice about a breast surgeon. As I got ready for bed, I felt something, a lump on my right breast. I thought to myself, Dr. S. felt the lump and didn't seem alarmed, there was nothing to worry about.

I looked over the list and called one of the breast surgeons she recommended the next day. This doctor wasn't accepting new patients until January 2018. I made my appointment for January 12th. What're three more weeks to wait?

I continued with my day to day routines, getting up at 5:15 a.m.; driving to work in Washington; DC; working at the U.S. Postal Service Headquarters. I enjoy my job, I have a passion for what I do, and that was helping others. On Sundays it was time for church at New Life Pentecostal in Ruther Glen, VA! It's a one-hour drive on Sunday mornings. Sunday evenings on the other hand was a different story, often a two-hour drive after church. I grew up in Ruther Glen, I'm blessed to hear my cousin, Bishop Thomas Holmes sing and preach the word! And did I say, HE CAN PREACH! When I left church, I spent time with my twin sister Carolyn, she is the nurturer of the family, I always stopped for a home cooked meal. I left home after college and moved to Northern VA, got married to my childhood boyfriend June 5, 1981, a month before my Dad died. Being a wife lasted 10 years; free, single and independent is a lot more fun.

Carolyn and her family lived at home and took care of Mom. She reminds me of Mom, she raised her two children like we were raised. In 2016 her son, Aubrey, moved into his own apartment in Fredericksburg, VA, a major accomplishment for a young 26 years old male. Her daughter Asia is a nurturer and caring person like her; outgoing and independent like me. She has been on her own since she left home for college in 2014. She graduated from Old Dominion University in December 2018. I am a proud Auntie!

Our family spent most of the day at the hospital with Mom on November 12, 2006, and left around 10 p.m., I was going to stay the night because my older sister, Libby who lives and raised her family in Washington, D.C., had stayed at the hospital with her the last few nights. I laid next to Mom and I whispered in her ear and reassured her, I would take care of the family. She closed her eyes and at 10:20 p.m. she took her last breath.

On January 1, 2018, I said to my sweetie, "I want to be engaged." We talked about how thankful we were to see 2018 and bring it in together. He suffered a medical scare a few months ago and is blessed that God healed his body. I said, yes that's what I want for 2018, to be engaged. I had no thoughts or plans of marriage because I still enjoy my independence. I asked him if he was okay with us being engaged, he laughed and said "Yes!" My engagement ring came from JARED and it is a beautiful ring! Proverbs 18:22 says, he who finds a wife finds a good thing, and obtains favor from the Lord. Even though I didn't wait for him to ask, God continues to bless me!

STAGE 2

January 12th, the breast surgeon and assistant entered the room. Not knowing what to expect. I was still nonchalant about this appointment. The mammogram results less than six months ago were all normal. He asked a few questions and said, "I want to do an ultrasound," which he did. Then he said, "I want to do a biopsy." He asked if I wanted to schedule it and come back. I said, "No, let's do it now." Let me tell you; I am a big crybaby when I see a needle! I asked, "Are you going to put me to sleep?" He said, "No, I will numb the area." I said to myself, "Oh my god, I don't know if I can do this." But I knew I did not want to come back to have it done either. I did it, the biopsy, and yes, I cried like a baby. The assistant held my hand through the entire procedure. I went back for the test results on January 19th, a week later. I thought little about the biopsy during the week; I wasn't worried. There is a saying or maybe it's a song, "if you pray don't worry, and if you worry, don't pray." I went into the same room the biopsy was done in. The doctor followed me in and waited for his assistant to enter. He sat down on the stool and she stood beside the door. He said, "The biopsy showed the lump was cancerous." He waited a couple of minutes, I assumed so I could digest what he said. He asked me, "Do you have any questions?" I said, "What stage would you say the cancer is?" He said, "Stage 1." He gave me a couple more seconds to digest that. He said, "I want you to schedule an MRI. Once you get yourself together, see the receptionist and make an appointment for the MRI." It's interesting, because I didn't need to get myself together, I didn't cry; I didn't ask a lot of questions; and I didn't need to get dressed. I think I was in shock or disbelief. I went to the receptionist, she gave me a list of instructions. She said, "You will get a call within 24 hours to schedule the MRI." She said, "You need to go to the imaging center where the mammogram was done and get a copy." She told me they needed the copy for their files. I said, "Excuse me," and she repeated everything. After that conversation with the receptionist, I walked out of the doctor's office shaking my head. January 19th was a Friday afternoon. I didn't get a call on Saturday or on Sunday, to schedule the MRI. I decided to get on the internet, and I googled the Cancer Treatment Centers of America (CTCA). They had 24/7 assistance, so I called the toll-free number and spoke to a cancer treatment center advocate. When I told her the reason for my call, she said: "I'm sorry to hear you have been diagnosed with breast cancer." She gathered my information and told me she would have a scheduler call me the next day.

On Monday, I was still waiting to hear from someone to schedule the MRI. I called the surgeon's office and said, "I thought someone was supposed to call me within 24 hours?" The receptionist said, "Oh you can call them." Again, shaking my head, I said, "really?" An hour later I got a call to schedule the MRI.

The earliest they could see me was February 2. I told the assistant, "I've contacted the CTCA for a second opinion." As soon as I hung up, I got a call from the CTCA scheduler and they asked, "How soon do you want to come in?" I said, "as soon as possible," the first available appointment was on January 31st. The next day CTCA emailed me my entire two-day schedule with names and occupations of all the doctors I would see. I was relieved I could have everything done at one location.

Deuteronomy 31:6 says, *"Be strong and of a good courage, fear not, nor be afraid of them: for the Lord thy God, it is He that doth go with thee; He will not fail thee, nor forsake thee"* (KJV).

I requested leave to be out of the office for 3 weeks. My mind was made up. I would stay in Philadelphia and do whatever I had to at the CTCA. I was not coming home until this cancerous lump was removed from my breast.

STAGE 3

Over the next several days, I prepared to go to Philly. Mentally, I was still in disbelief; I didn't tell my family. I didn't want them to worry, which is what they would have done. This was my journey, it was a test of my faith, and the only person I wanted with me was God. It was going to be okay; I trusted God. I said to myself, I would tell my family after meeting with the doctors. I wanted my focus to be on God, my relationship with Him; and to build one with the doctors. That would have been hard to do with family and friends around. I called my pastor, Tommy, on Wednesday, five days before I left to go to Philly. I told him I was diagnosed with breast cancer, I asked him to pray for me that night at bible study. The one thing I knew for sure is with pastor sending up prayers for me, everything was going to be alright. He's said before, "You have to be careful who you ask to pray for you." On Sunday, January 28th the prayers continued during morning service. I was in the house of the Lord; I could feel Gods presence! Pastor and I touched and agreed, God was in control. He sung, There's a Miracle in This Room, With Your Name on It, by Tarsha Cobbs. I felt the Holy Spirit moving, and I believe everyone in church felt it too! I know God is a healer! Psalms 55:22 says, *"Give your burdens to the Lord, and he will take care of you. He will not permit the godly to slip and fall"* (NLV). I laid my burdens down and left them at the altar! I stopped by the house to see Carolyn before heading home. We ate and reminisced about back in the day. She and I laughed, I couldn't believe I use to sing in the choir. We agreed, I can't sing. We sang this one song, "glory glory, hallelujah, since I laid my burdens down; I feel better, so much better, since I laid my burdens down." We loved Sunday school and church, as kids we had no worries growing up. We had a good life, we grew up in loving homes, with hard working parents who loved us unconditionally. We got our butts whipped often when we acted up. I decided to tell Carolyn I was heading to Philly on Tuesday for doctor's appointments. I said to her, "I have breast cancer." She said, "Why am I just hearing about this?" I told her I didn't want her worrying and getting sick. I said, "Gods got this." She said, "I'm going with you." I knew she would say that. I told her, I didn't want anyone with me but GOD! She didn't understand why I didn't tell her and was going alone. I called my cousin Loretta who is a five-year breast cancer survivor, I put her on speaker phone. I said, "I need you to be here to support Carolyn. I have breast cancer and I need you to be with her; talk to her and help her understand why I've made these decisions. Loretta was there for her and she encouraged Carolyn to trust, believe and have faith. I know my twin, she feels my pain and I feel hers; she would have worried herself sick about me. I had no worries, God is a healer and would not leave or forsake me now; I knew He would be with me.

I put my headset on, and I listened to my gospel CD, Timeless by the Williams Brothers, as I took the two-hour train ride to Philly from Union Station on January 30th. It was my first time on Amtrak, the trip was so peaceful. A driver from CTCA met me at Penn Station and took me to my hotel. I had no stress, CTCA made all the arrangements.

Everyone was so nice. I met with my own dedicated team of doctors, a primary care, surgeon, reconstructive surgeon, radiologist, oncologist, and genetics doctor, as scheduled and then a chiropractor, physical and occupational therapist. Where else can you see all these doctors in one location? I went from one appointment to the next. They were all waiting for me, I felt like they already knew me. Each one was well informed, they had already reviewed my chart by the time I went in to see them. A very organized team and they had answers to all my questions.

Carol Wright

After seeing all the doctors, my surgeon asked me, "Carol what do you want to do"? I said, "Based on all the doctors' opinions and the 3D mammogram you scheduled, that still did not detect the lump, I am having a double mastectomy, because if the mammogram did not detect the lump in my right breast, it's possible I could have one in my left." I said, "I'm not taking any chances, remove both breast; I'm only going through this once." Then I told him, "I'm not having reconstructive surgery either." Dr. S. said, "I think that's a good idea." He asked me, "When do you want to have the surgery?" I said, "Tomorrow," then I thought about it, "No let's not have it tomorrow, its super bowl weekend; Philadelphia is playing, and I want to enjoy the game!" I told him I was in Philly for a reason and they were going to win because I am here. He laughed, looked at his schedule and said, "What about Monday, February 5th," I said, "Monday it is." He promised me he would not be up to late partying and enjoying the super bowl.

I got on an earlier shuttle and arrived at CTCA early for my surgery. I sat in the waiting room relaxing, listening to gospel music on my phone. I called my cousin, Bishop Holmes and asked him to pray for and with me. We prayed and agreed! God is still in control, He was going to perform a miracle; please guide the surgeon's hands; there is healing in the name of Jesus; I would be healed in Jesus Name. I woke up in recovery a few hours later. I sat in bed, the nurses asked, "how do you feel?" I said, "I feel fine."

My sister, called around 5 p.m., and fussed at me, "Why didn't you call to let us know you were okay?" I'd given the receptionist instructions to call my family. Not sure what happened to my message. Carolyn could hear in my voice that I was okay, she wanted me to send her a picture so she could see for herself. I laughed!

Dr. S. came by at 6 p.m. to check on me, he said, "the surgery went well, it was 2 ½ hours long and that my stitches looked good." He said, "You will be released tomorrow." I said I could stay another day, just in case. He asked, "Are you in any pain?" I said, "No", he told me I was going home.

The next day I relaxed on the 2 p.m. train from Penn to Union Station. My good friends Gail and Ron met me at the train station. I was home and in bed by 6 p.m., one day after having a double mastectomy, it was still hard to believe! Early, the next morning, I sent my brother Kirk a text message and pictures of me in my room after the surgery and asked him to call me. Carolyn, my cousin Loretta, and her brother Tommy, my pastor, were on their way to make sure I was okay and to take care of me. Tommy worked at National Airport and dropped them off at my house for a couple of days. I called my sister's cell to see if they were on their way. She asked, "How do you feel?" I said, "I feel so good I can't stand myself!" They all laughed, but I was serious. I had no pain whatsoever! I did not look like what I had been through. That was evident when Carolyn and Loretta walked though my front door. They couldn't believe, I was up, dressed, face made up, and greeted them with a gigantic smile. I laughed and said, "I sent you all pictures yesterday after surgery." Well, it looks like I only sent the pictures to Tommy, he stood back and laughed at us. They cooked for me, they cleaned the kitchen, washed cloths, and took very good care of me. I enjoyed their company, but I told Tommy to pick them up Thursday; on his way home, after he got off from work. They said I kicked them out...I did! Kirk and his wife Shelia drove up from Richmond to check on me too.

STAGE 4

I went back to the CTCA on February 19th, for my follow-up appointments. When my surgeon was ready to remove the drain tubes inserted in my chest, right under the area where I use to have breast, I said, "It's not going to hurt is it?" "I don't like pain." He said, "I don't either, I'll count to three, one." I took a deep breath, and it was out on the count of one. I laugh about it now! The doctors were so good, I never experienced any pain. He told me I was cancer free! My Oncologist explained the different types of treatment plans and explained the pathology report. I agreed to a Genomics test to see how aggressive the cancer was. I'll would come back for my next appointment in 30 days, the test should be ready then. I stopped by my office when I got to DC and gave my VP and manager and update. They saw my happiness! I couldn't help but be happy and thankful, look at what the Lord has done for me. I was just told I was cancer free! My VP said, "You are not coming back, are you?" I told her no, I don't think I am coming back to work.

Carol Wright

STAGE 5

A friend called, she asked if she could give my information to a coworker who was just diagnosed with breast cancer. When I told her and other friends, I had breast cancer, I asked them not to tell others. I was the only one who could tell my story and I wanted friends and family to hear it from me. I said, "sure, give her my cell number." I asked, "who is it?" I couldn't believe it, it was one of my friends. I didn't wait for her to call me, I called her. I asked if we could meet for lunch or dinner to talk. I came to the job and picked her up and we went to lunch in the park. I told her my story and experience at the CTCA. Before we finished lunch, we called and made her appointments. I told her I would go with her if she wanted me to. When I got home, I took a picture of my schedule and texted the information to her. She had the same team of doctors.

A few day later, I decided to reach out to family and friends through Facebook and Instagram. I wanted my family to know I had breast cancer and to share information with them. By sharing my story, I found out that at least 10 family members had cancer. I would have done the genetic testing if I had known this before my surgery. Kirk had two sons, Andre and Travis.

Andre died of cancer at age 32, after a 10-year battle. My aunt and several cousins' loss their battle with cancer also. CTCA has a huge fish tank with the most beautiful fish and starfish. I gave each fish a name of a family member or friend who had passed or had suffered with cancer. I named the starfish Andre, he was like a shining star; he was always encouraging others. We have to educate the next generation, so they are aware of the effects of cancer in our family.

I contacted my Human Resources Office and requested my retirement paperwork. I hadn't been to work in two months. I'd enjoyed the time off, I needed it to strengthen and heal my body and to continue my very personal relationship with God. I am so blessed; God prepared me for cancer! Gratitude is my attitude and I have an attitude of gratitude with unspeakable joy. My steps were ordered, God had a plan for me, and He doesn't make any mistakes. He is a faithful God, He was with me on this journey and will walk along beside me through it all. Hebrews 13:5 says, *"Let your conversation be without covetousness; and be content with such things as ye have: for he hath said, I will never leave thee, nor forsake."* (KJV)

STAGE 6

On March 25, 2018, I was baptized again by my cousin Tommy at our church, New Life Pentecostal, and rededicated my life to God. Psalm 34 says, *"I will bless the Lord at all times: his praise shall continually be in my mouth. My soul shall make her boast in the Lord; the humble shall hear thereof and be glad. O magnify the Lord with me and let us exalt his name together. I sought the Lord, and he heard me, and delivered me from all my fears."* (KJV).

I believed and I trusted God. In April, I retired and put my condo on the market. In June, I moved to North Carolina. Two days after moving I enjoyed vacationing on a seven-day cruise in Alaska and sightseeing in Vancouver!

What's next? I don't know, but I look forward to God's plan for ME! So, stay tuned! I do know that because of **ME, MY FAITH, AND GOD'S FAVOR**...HE will continue to direct my footsteps.

My life has been changed! What a difference 30 days made! I kicked cancers' A$$ in 30 days!

Me, My Faith and God's Favor

Carol Wright

My name is Carol Nelson Wright, I am a breast cancer survivor!

I have a strong faith in God and have the favor of God's grace on my life.

If it had not been for the Lord on my side through this journey, I would not be wearing this T-shirt that says: Strong, Brave, Fierce! I am that woman.

I walk by faith and not by sight, I'm excited to see what God has planned for me!

Carol Wright

Contact

Email: authorcarolwright@gmail.com

Facebook: MsCarol Wright

Acknowledgements

I give God all the praise and the glory.

I would like to acknowledge my twin sister Carolyn who has always been right by my side through thick and thin. She feels my pain and I feel hers; that's the closeness and bond we've shared since birth. I love you so much!

To my brother Kirk, a strong determined man, who has always worked hard to support his family. I admire that so much in you! You will continue to be blessed because of the man you are; you are just like our Dad and brother Winnie.

My cousin, Tommy, thank you for teaching me the Word of God at New Life Pentecostal Church. Because of your faithfulness, God has blessed you abundantly with favor. I know that I'm blessed because of you, our church family, and God. Thank you for praying with me just before I went into surgery, I know God heard your prayer request for a miracle. I am a living witness!

He placed so many angels in my path along this journey, my cousin Loretta, my fiancé Rolando and best friends, Gerri, Yolanda, Bertha, and Joie.

There were some unintended angels, like Milan who came in on her day off, to color my hair, before I went to Philly. I thank the Lord for my surgeon Dr. S. and my CTCA cancer support team Mary and Bernice. Arika, a ticket clerk at Union Station who took a beautiful starfish pendent off her neck and placed it around mine. Read the Starfish Poem below to understand why this made me cry.

"Once upon a time, there was a wise man who used to go to the ocean to do his writing. He had a habit of walking on the beach before he began his work.

One day, as he was walking along the shore, he looked down the beach and saw a human figure moving like a dancer. He smiled to himself at the thought of someone who would dance to the day, and so, he walked faster to catch up.

Carol Wright

As he got closer, he noticed that the figure was that of a young man, and that what he was doing was not dancing at all. The young man was reaching down to the shore, picking up small objects, and throwing them into the ocean.

He came closer still and called out "Good morning! May I ask what it is that you are doing?"

The young man paused, looked up, and replied "Throwing starfish into the ocean."

"I must ask, then, why are you throwing starfish into the ocean?" asked the somewhat startled wise man.

To this, the young man replied, "The sun is up and the tide is going out. If I don't throw them in, they'll die."

Upon hearing this, the wise man commented, "But, young man, do you not realize that there are miles and miles of beach and there are starfish all along every mile? You can't possibly make a difference!"

Me, My Faith and God's Favor

At this, the young man bent down, picked up yet another starfish, and threw it into the ocean. As it met the water, he said,
"It made a difference for that one."
— Loren Eiseley

And last but certainly not least, to all my family and friends, you know who you are, thank you for your support, I love you guys. I pray that God will continue to bless you and your families! Have faith and let the Lord direct your footsteps, as He has done for me, in Jesus Name I pray, Amen!

Patricia Fowler
LOVE DON'T LEAVE YOU BRUISED

I want to share with you my experience with Domestic Violence and how it was only by the grace of God that I am here today to talk, share and educate other women on its effects.

First John 4:18 says, *"There is no fear in love; but perfect love casteth out fear because fear hath torment. He that feareth is not made perfect in love."* This is not a situation you should be in. This is why as single women; we must wait on God for our mates. Yes, I know it may seem like everyone else is dating and in relationships, but that does not mean that it is the perfect or the right relationship You cannot base what's going on or what's not going on in your life compared to your girlfriend's life. What God has for you is for you. Exhibit the fruit of the spirit with patience and wait on what and who God has for you.

I met the love of my life at the age of 25. I was introduced to him by a family member. I thought we were in love. He asked me to marry him like three times and I said no. When he asked me again, I said

Love Don't Leave You Bruised

yes. We dated for two years and he was everything I could imagine in a man and husband and more. I believed in God at the time, but I was not technically saved, and neither was he. I married him at the age of 27. Once we got married and after we had our first child, things started to change. The person who I thought I knew and loved was changing right before my eyes. The man who never cursed, who brought me flowers all the time, who spoiled me with gifts now was yelling at me, putting his hands on me, making me cry, making me feel like I was nothing. He was living like he was single and not married with a family.

Then one day it happened, the abuse started, which led to black eyes, embarrassment on my job and in public. Harsh ridicule about my looks after birthing our children, being left alone, infidelity and more.

During the marriage, I lived walking on egg shells for a long time because, I knew if he had a bad day or was drinking that it was going to be a fight or screaming and yelling. I over compensated in trying to be the best wife and mother that I could, but some days that was just not good enough for him. I remember days when I came home from work, cooked dinner, bathed and fed the children and put them to bed, had his dinner ready and then I would get yelled at because I cooked something he did not want!! It got to the point that I was so scared of what he would do that even when we were in the car riding, I would keep my head down and not look around because if he saw me looking at a car with a man in it, he would accuse me of wanting that man. I recall one day I came home and spoke to my male neighbor and was accused of messing around with him and all I did was say hi after he spoke to me.

I recall one day that I was on the balcony of our apartment and it was some men on the balcony across from us. He saw those men on that balcony and it sent him into a frenzy. He accused me of watching and wanting them and in return he kicked our balcony glass door out. It's funny that if he saw a man hitting on a woman, he would break it up, but at the same time he was doing the same thing to me.

Sometimes someone can mentally and emotionally abuse you to the point that you really can't think for

Love Don't Leave You Bruised

yourself. Sometimes I felt like I did not know who I was because everything I did was based off of what I thought needed to happen according to his mood. No one should live in fear of just being themselves.

Imagine you having a child for the man you love and live with and afterwards, he calls you a fat pig!! Yes, I experienced this. It's such a hurtful feeling when you think the person who says they love you can also put you down in so many ways. I was taunted about my baby weight. After that I started getting myself together and working towards losing the weight. In doing so, I got very small again as in my earlier days I was tiny. At that point, I was then accused of cheating on him with someone at my place of employment because I was dressing up and going to get my hair done, but I was just trying to please my husband, so he could start loving me again. I kept telling myself if someone love's you, they won't leave you bruised.

I recall one Christmas I had a black eye. I don't remember what the fight was about, but I do recall my two small sons seeing it and of course, I lied to them and said that I hit the cabinet. I wrote a poem behind

Patricia Fowler

that called "Black Eyes and Cries," no mother should ever have to hide bruises or lie to their children about something their father did.

BLACK EYES AND CRIES

Another black eye, a busted lip and an injured hip
God is so good to me anyway,
I ain't even going to trip

He did this to me again for no good reason or rhyme
If he has been drinking, it's sure to happen every time

I had better walk normal,
Talk to no one about my lil trip
Still have to get up and go to work tomorrow,
Can't let it slip

Stand up straight and tall, and don't even try to limp
Always looking over my shoulders with every glimpse

Looking at my kids as I tuck them into their beds
Little one says Oh Mommy,
What happened to your head?
Oh, baby mommy fell while cleaning and

Love Don't Leave You Bruised

I hit the wall
Baby boy replies that must have been a really hard fall

Trying to hide and not let anyone know or see my real pain

Keeping it bottled up to myself,
I had no self-esteem to claim

He thought I was down and out,
And just at the end of my rope
With faith the size of a mustard seed, there was still some hope

I am an angel in heaven looking down on family daily you see
It's sad my life ended like this
When I knew they prayed for me

Family I'm ok, so please know that everything is well
Even though I'm gone, you all still have a story to tell.

There were periods during our marriage that things were not so bad, but I recall of lot of bad times as well. I recall one day my husband was mad, and I don't remember about what, but I recall he came up to my place of employment and he was yelling at me and made a scene. I was so scared that I just sat there with my head held down and my co-workers were just kind of looking as they were not sure what to do. I did not say anything because I knew that would send him over even more, so I just let him finish and he left.

I believe that most women think that when they meet "Mr. Right", get married, have a family and are living life together it's supposed to be a happy time. A time of reflection on the good things that brought us together and how we are growing as one and a family. But imagine being married and still feeling like you are single. Imagine living in depression and your spouse does not even know it. Imagine wanting to kill yourself, but the only thing that stopped you is the fact that you pictured your children's faces at the attempt. Imagine that one day you and your spouse are fighting physically, and you call the police, but while doing so he snatches the phone out the wall. Usually when you dial 911 by mistake or kids playing on the phone, they will usually call back or even come because they can trace the address. Well, I called and when he pulled the

Love Don't Leave You Bruised

plug out, nothing happened. They did not call or come and at this point I realized that I could be have severely injured.

I recall one night I was at home with the kids, which I did very often, and my husband had gone out. We had a dog at the time. When my husband got home, he saw that the dog had been sick on the floor and he woke me up and started fighting with me because I had not cleaned it up. Well, if I was sleep, I did not even know this had taken place. When a person is angry, or their mood and mind is altered by alcohol it is no telling what can happen at any given moment day or night.

I have a lot of memories of things that happened that were bad, but since that time I have chosen to be forgiving so that I can move on with my life and not live in the past.

After much prayer to God and the Holy Spirit telling me to get out, I would not be here today had I not listened to the Lord. It was not an easy decision, but I knew that if I did not leave, that I would probably have been killed. I encourage any woman at the first sign of abuse, to get out and get help. Think of yourself, think of your children. God did not create you to be killed or beaten by someone who claims to love you. Be patient and wait on the Lord because **LOVE DON'T LEAVE YOU BRUISED**!! After 10 years, I got out. I trusted God to lead me to a life of not being abused, taken for granted, treated badly and all that abuse entails. Today, I am still single, celibate, happy and have found myself in Jesus and I commend you to do the same if this is your testimony. I will continue to talk about Domestic Violence because making someone else aware is key to their freedom!!!

A lot of women in their lives may have met the man who they thought was their Knight in Shining Armor. That guy that we have met whether at the store, at the bank or he was introduced to us by a mutual friend. We saw so much good in him that he could do no wrong at all. This is the person that I was going to marry and live my life with and have a couple of babies, we would have a big house in the city, and he would take care of us forever.

Love Don't Leave You Bruised

The reality of the above is not that it can't happen, but when we think it is happening, it's not. The scripture in the bible says when a man finds a wife, he finds a good thing and obtains favor from the Lord. As women, we have to be careful of who we connect ourselves to. Just because someone is handsome, has a job and a nice fancy car, does not mean he is the one for us or the man of our dreams. If a man truly wants to be your knight in shining armor, then he will come to you in the proper way. He will be a man of God, fearfully and wonderfully made, so that he will recognize and realize that he has something special and will treat you as such.

A man that knows the true value of a woman will not disrespect her and treat her like she is worthless. A real man knows how to appreciate the queen he has been blessed with, but a man whose mind is not stayed on God won't understand that to her, he is her everything. He is her knight in shining armor. He can make all things better. He will take care of whatever issues arise in the relationship, marriage and household.

Patricia Fowler

I understand why some women stay in these bad situations, just as I did for years. However, today's society has so much to offer victims of abuse and there is so much awareness and resources open to you to help you be well educated on these matters.

Don't allow an unreal moment to make you believe that just because of a gentle kiss on the forehead and some kind words that he will not put his hands on you again or that it is going I change without getting any help. It's all a part of the trap they pull you into thinking that they are sorry for what they did. Again, no matter what excuses they give you, you have to remember **LOVE DON'T LEAVE YOU BRUISED**.

A forehead kiss cannot take way the pain and hurt of a black eye or a broken arm. A forehead kiss cannot bring back the baby that you miscarried by your abuser beating you. A forehead kiss cannot replace the teeth he knocked out because you talked back to him. So, I say to you, beautiful woman, do not allow the kiss of death to lull and you back into the arms of a person who does not value you or your life.

Love Don't Leave You Bruised

If you are a woman who has been in a domestic violence relationship or whether you have never endured a situation like mine, I believe that it is important for you to know and be able to recognize the acts of violence that comes with an abuser treating you as if you were a punching bag. Please see the list below to make yourself aware so if you ever encounter any of these things you can be warned about the acts of violence:

- Pushing
- Slapping
- Kicking
- Grabbing poking
- Choking
- Breaking bones
- Punching
- Pulling hair
- Twisting arms
- Taking belongings
- Controlling whereabouts

Although there are many more red flags to look for and be aware of, I think it boils down to being careful that your mate is God sent!!! In waiting on God, you can almost be sure that you will not endure these problems. When you see things that are not right or out of order, please do not ignore what you are seeing as it will only get worse as time goes on. I myself never thought I would endure something like this, nor did I think or want my marriage to be over. Had I or my husband and I gone to counseling, perhaps we could have salvaged the marriage, but that was not the case in my story. However, I am here to share with you so that you will not go down that same road I did.

The Bible says in Proverbs 24:1-2, *"Do not envy wicked men do not desire their company for their hearts plot violence and their lips talk about making trouble."*

When you are threatened by your abuser, believe him and do not allow yourself to stay in that environment any longer. Once you have been given the tools and signs to look for you are well equipped, so that if it happens you know what to do. Too often women blame themselves for the bad way's men treat us. However, it is NEVER a woman's fault. A man that hits a woman is not a real man. Inside this man is dealing with something that has happened to him in his past that he has not dealt with.

Proverbs 3:15 states *"She is more precious than rubies; nothing you desire can compare with her."* Do you know that rubies are the most expensive gem in the world? Why would you want or allow someone to damage them? As women, we should know that we are like rubies.

You have to know your true value!!!!!! You are a Women of Worth!!

Overcoming domestic violence is not an easy task. Today we hear of so many people who have been in domestic violence situations and/or many that still are and then there are those that don't make it out, but they end up losing their lives due to the violence. This is one of the main reasons I advocate for domestic violence awareness and prevention because I want to educate anyone I can. When I was going through it, I did not have anyone to talk to, nor did I know about any 1-800 number like they have today. And often when you go to the abuser's family, they do not understand and will not support you. The most important part of domestic violence is knowing the warning signs so that you can avoid it. It is also key to note that your mate should be sent to you from God and not someone you have chosen on your own. The bible says, *"He who finds a wife, finds a good thing and obtains favor from the Lord."*

Out of everything I have said here, the one valuable lesson that I would like you to take away is that someone can only do to you what you allow. When you know who you are and whose you are, you will not accept just anything. Don't settle!! Some think being single is a curse, but I beg to differ. Since I've been single, I have learned a lot about myself. I have learned more about the Lord Jesus and how He protects me, I have experienced traveling and exploring different things as well as working on myself to be better person and continue to grow in the Lord.

One of the hardest things about domestic violence is breaking your silence. As long as you are quiet, your abuser can continue to violate you and possibly end up taking your life. I am glad that my life was spared by the Glory of God, but I also want to encourage you so

Love Don't Leave You Bruised

that yours can be spared as well. Please repeat these confessions each day to remind you that **LOVE DON'T LEAVE YOU BRUISED** and anything to the contrary is not of God.

Confessions

I am important and my life matters!!
I was not created to be abused in any way!!
I will not tolerate control issues of any kind!!
I will not settle just to say I have a man!!
I will not keep quiet if I'm hurt or battered!!
I will not stay in a bad relationship!!
I will not take legal action, then drop it!!
I won't keep secrets from family and friends!!

I will not subject my child(dren) to abuse!!
I will not ignore the red flags!!

LOVE DON'T LEAVE YOU BRUISED!!!!!

Black Eyes and Cries is dedicated to any woman who has experienced domestic Violence.

Patricia Fowler

Patricia Fowler

Patricia Fowler is an Advocate, Author, Minister of the Gospel and Speaker. She is the founder of "Pure Heart Ministries." She is a survivor of Domestic Violence and advocate. Patricia speaks on her past experience with domestic violence in hopes of helping other women to feel free enough to speak on their situations to get out and get help.

Patricia uses her past experience as a married woman in an ungodly and abusive relationship to help guide and mentor other young women. She became a first time Author, December 2017 with her first

Love Don't Leave You Bruised

inspirational book titled *Strength in Her Struggles*. She is now a Co-Author with her second book titled *Relentless Pursuit* which speaks directly to her journey with Domestic Violence and sharing what love is according to the Bible.

Contact

For bookings & engagements, please contact her at:
Phone: 540-272-6150
Email: pureheartministries2@gmail.com
Web: www.pureheart-ministries.com
Facebook: Evangelist Trisha Fowler
Instagram: Evangelist Trisha
Twitter: @EvangelistTrysh

LaKesha L. Williams

TRIUMPHANT OVERCOMERS

It is my desire that as a result of reading this book, an awareness has been awakened in you and a boldness has been activated within you that you can triumph over hardship. Some of the stories that have been shared in this book are really just snippets of things these **TRIUMPHANT OVERCOMERS** have experienced. They shared their stories in hopes that they would be the catalyst to initiate a chain reaction of hope and a sense of superhero-ness through Jesus Christ in your life. What I mean is any and everything that happens to you or that you are currently going through in your life should illicit a response of peace because you know God has equipped you to emerge from suffering triumphantly.

I am a summation of everything I have ever experienced in my entire 36 years of life. Every hurt, every pain, every joy, every happy moment, every worry and every doubt have all been orchestrated by God. Before I was born, God had written my story. He knew me—my purpose, He knew; my pain, He knew; He knew what I would be like, who I would be, what I would like and dislike, and who my family, friends, and associates would be. He knew my purpose before I knew me, and He knew that through His Son Jesus, I would be equipped to overcome the tragedies that He would allow to come my way in this world!

Merriam Webster defines the word 'purpose' as the reason for which something exists or is done, made or used. God created you and I for and with a purpose. God created you and I for a reason. We exist because God wants us to, God needs us to fulfill His purposes in this Earth. Genesis 1:31 (NLT) says, *"Then God looked over all He had made and He saw that it was very good!"* Guess who was a part of this "very good" creation? If you said, "I am!" you're correct!!

Genesis 1:31 (NLT) tells us God saw that all He had created was excellent in every way. You are a part of God's creation and He is pleased with how He made you. If at times you feel worthless or of little value, remember that God made you for a good reason. You are valuable to Him. Now I know what you are thinking, for many, this is a hard concept to grasp with all that we experience in our lives. And honestly, I didn't always believe I was valuable to Him myself. But God relentlessly pursues those whom He has called and chosen!

I am sure that my life is not too different from yours. I am also sure that many of you can relate in some way; or know how someone who can relate: to the stories you've read in this collaboration. I know I can! My life has been full of questions, especially in the midst of suffering. All of us have a tendency to ask questions such as "What is my purpose? Why was I created? How do I fit into God's bigger picture? Why do I experience the things that I do or have? How do I overcome these things? How or will I emerge triumphantly over this situation or circumstance and how can I bring glory to God and be a contribution to this world?" Now don't get too excited because I cannot answer any of these questions for you, but I can share how I arrived at an answer for myself, which I believe will be encouraging and inspiring to you.

In 2013 I turned 30 years old and it has become a tradition amongst my family and friends that, on our birthday we share what we have learned over the past year and how God has blessed us. During my 30th

Triumphant Overcomers

Birthday celebration dinner, I decided to share my testimony with a few of my closest family and friends. This was the first time that I had shared my full testimony with any of them, including my mother who was present. As I was sharing my testimony, God revealed something very powerful to me:

He revealed that everything I have experienced in life (the good, the bad, and the horribly ugly) was so that I could bring glory, honor, and fame to His Name.

Wait, what, hold up! Yes, you read that right! It's not about me and it's not about you…it's about God, His glory and bringing Him fame! That is how we truly live as **TRIUMPHANT OVERCOMERS**. Exodus 9:16 (NLT) says, *"But I have spared you for a purpose, to show you My power and to spread My fame throughout the earth."* I have been in situations where I could have been killed, ended up in jail or ended up insane, BUT GOD spared me because HE had a purpose for my life. He had a purpose for my story, He had a purpose in the stories you have read in this book and He knew that all that I have ever experienced since the day of my birth would bring Him Glory and Fame.

That is so powerful, that tidbit alone is life changing. Knowing that God has a purpose for you even when life is hard, even when you feel like God has forgotten about you, when you are experiencing the worst pain or heartache that you think you could endure, God has not forgotten about you nor has God forsaken you.

GOD HAS NOT FORGOTTEN ABOUT YOU!

GOD HAS NOT FORSAKEN YOU!

God created you with a purpose and a plan, to help others through sharing your stories and lead others into the knowledge of Him.

Romans 8:28-29 (NLT) says, *"And we know that God causes everything to work together for the good of those who love God and are called according to His purpose for them. [29]For God knew His people in advance and He chose them to become like His Son, so that His Son would be the firstborn among many brothers and sisters."* This verse embodies what God revealed to me on my 30th birthday, everything I have ever been through, everything I have ever experienced, everything that has ever been done

Triumphant Overcomers

to me and every tear that I have ever cried was not for naught. This verse alone tells me many things about myself and about the life I have lived and have yet to live. This verse tells me that no matter what, I am a **TRIUMPHANT OVERCOMER** and guess what, so are you!

God works in "all things" - not just isolated incidents – for our good. This does not mean that all that happens to us is good. Evil is prevalent in our fallen world, but God is able to turn every circumstance around for our long-range good. Note that God is not working to make us happy, but to fulfill His purpose. Note also that this promise is not for everybody. It can be claimed only by those who love God and are called according to His purpose. Those who are "called" are those the Holy Spirit convinces and enables to receive Christ. Such people have a new perspective, a new mindset on life. They trust in God, not life's treasures; they look for their security in heaven, not on earth; they learn to accept, not resent, pain and persecution because God is with them.

Romans 8:28-29 (NLT) also tells me that if I love God, He will work everything out (the good, the bad and the horribly ugly), for my good. Which means no matter what happens to me God can use it or use me as a result of experiencing it. This verse also tells me that I am called according to God's purpose. That piece of the scripture is encouraging in and of itself, but you may be thinking, "If God has a purpose for me why do I have to suffer, why does my life at times seem so hard?" I have asked myself that very same question on numerous occasions. The answer can be found in verse 29 where it says, *"For God knew His people in advance and He chose them to become like His Son...."* God chose you to be like His Son, Jesus and Jesus suffered much. Jesus was God's only Begotten Son and He suffered for a purpose. God loved Jesus and He loves us, so why would you expect not to suffer? The good news is, although Jesus suffered much; Jesus also overcame much so just like God chose you to be like His Son, God chose you to endure, so like Jesus you can emerge triumphantly!

God's ultimate goal for us is to make us like Christ. First John 3:2 (NASB) says, *"Beloved, now we are children of God, and it has not appeared as yet what we will be. We know that when He appears, we will be like Him, because we will see Him just as He is."* The Christian life is a process of becoming mre and more like Christ. This process will not be complete until we see Christ face-to-face. In the meantime, as we become more and more like Him, we discover our true selves, the persons we were created to be. How can we be conformed to Christ's likeness? By reading and heeding the Word, by studying His life on earth through the Gospels, by being filled with His Spirit and by doing His work in the world.

More proof:

Before I formed you in the womb, I knew you and before you were born, I set you apart; I appointed you as a Prophet to the nations.
Jeremiah 1:5 (NLT)

In Jeremiah 1:5 (NLT), God gave Jeremiah a message. God told Jeremiah that He knew him before He formed him in his mother's womb, before he was even born and probably before his mother was born or thought about, God had already appointed Jeremiah as a Prophet to the nations.

God knew you, as He knew Jeremiah, long before you were born or even conceived. He thought about you and planned for you. When you feel discouraged or inadequate, remember that God has always thought of you as valuable and that He has a purpose in mind for you.

This verse if full of promise and hope! Think about that for a moment, this verse starts out saying *"Before I formed you in the womb, I knew you....,"* so you mean to tell me, before my parents knew each other, before they were married or even thought about having children, God knew me? Wow isn't that an awesome thought, God knew you, and He took the time to form you in your mother's womb!

The next part of the verse is just as good, it says *"...before you were born I set you apart...."* If you research the words "set apart" you will find something very interesting, the words "set apart" are connected to the word holiness. According to Merriam Webster, the word holiness is a noun that means "state or character of being holy." Holy is also an adjective that means "belonging to, derived from or associated with a divine power" and also "set apart to the service of God." In other words, that which is holy belongs to God. It is sanctified, meaning "set apart for a holy use or purpose." How can someone who is set apart for a holy use or purpose not be created to live triumphantly, those two things simply don't go together.

Before you were born, God deemed you as holy, He set you apart for His holy use and purpose, how awesome is that? Psalms 139:16 (NLT) says, *"You saw me before I was born. Every day of my life was recorded in your book. Every moment was laid out before a single day had passed."* God created you and I with a purpose, you did not enter this world just because your parents hooked up and conceived you; your introduction to this world was predestined and predesigned by God Himself. God did not bring you into this world just to suffer and experience tragedies.

In the last part of Jeremiah 1:5, in God's message to Jeremiah He lets him know exactly what his purpose is, it says, *"I appointed you as a Prophet to the nations."* Before Jeremiah was born and even before the foundation of this Earth, God knew him, God had set him apart and God had appointed him.

God has a purpose for each Christian, but some people are appointed by God for specific kinds of work. Samson, David, John the Baptist and Paul were also called to do particular jobs for God. Whatever work you do should be done for the Glory of God. If God gives you a specific task, accept it cheerfully and do it with diligence. If God has not given you a specific call or assignment, then seek to fulfill the mission common to all believers – to love, obey and serve God – until His guidance becomes clearer.

Now I want you to take Jeremiah's name out of the scripture and insert your name or an "I" and say it aloud:

"Before I was born and even before the foundation of the Earth, God knew me, God set me apart and God appointed me."

Isn't that powerful, isn't that encouraging, I must admit I have not always believed the above statement, and that is what this book is about. This book is about the promise that God placed on our lives before we were even born, actually before our parents were born. We all were born with a promise and for a purpose, and that promise, and that purpose is proof from God that we are **TRIUMPHANT OVERCOMERS**.

Before the purpose and the promise comes the pain and the process of overcoming Satan's attacks. The pain is what you have to go through and endure in life for God to develop, grow and transform you, this is the stage where we may or may not know God or have a close relationship with Him so everything in life seems hard and we constantly ask "Why me?" and feel sorry for ourselves, our situations and our circumstances.

The process begins when we realize that everything in our lives that has occurred has happened for a reason. This is the time that we begin to look beyond our lives, beyond our little world and see God's bigger picture. Think of it this way, our lives are like 4x6 pictures, all we see in our own picture is ourselves, our problems, our worries, our family, our jobs, and our friends and so on. But God's picture is so big that I cannot put a number on it and our little 4x6 picture is just one very small part of His big picture. When you think in those terms, you begin to see that although our picture is small, we fit into God's picture, we have a place. When your perspective changes, you will begin to walk in and fulfill the promise that God has placed on your life.

I want you to be encouraged by what you have read in these pages and I also want you to be reminded that with God anybody can live triumphantly. There is a **TRIUMPHANT OVERCOMER** inside all of us!!!

Triumphant Overcomers

LaKesha L. Williams

ARE YOU A TRIUMPHANT OVERCOMER?

For His Spirit joins with our spirit to affirm that we are God's children. And since we are His children, we are His heirs. In fact, together with Christ, we are heirs of God's glory. But if we are to share His glory, we must also share His suffering. Yet what we suffer now is nothing compared to the glory He will reveal to us later.
Romans 8:16-18

John 16:33 says, *"These things I have spoken to you, so that in Me you may have peace. In the world you have tribulation but take courage; I have overcome the world."* With these words, Jesus told His disciples to take courage because, despite the inevitable struggles they would face, they would not be alone, as you have seen through the testimonies you have just read. Jesus does not abandon us to our struggles either. If we remember that the ultimate victory has already been won, we can claim the peace of following Christ. Jesus was unmistakably confident that the choice to follow Him would not be easy or free from struggle.

Are you a Triumphant Overcomer?

First John 5:4-5 says, *"For whatever is born of God overcomes the world; and this is the victory that has overcome the world—our faith. Who is the one who overcomes the world, but he who believes that Jesus is the Son of God?"*

Are you living like a **TRIUMPHANT OVERCOMER**? The very process of overcoming implies that there is a struggle. The beauty of the struggle is becoming a **TRIUMPHANT OVERCOMER**. God wants to use the struggle to push you towards Him.

The key is to take on the spirit of a **TRIUMPHANT OVERCOMER** and "come over" those mountains that you face. Galatians 6:9 reveals the profile of a **TRIUMPHANT OVERCOMER**, *"Let us not lose heart in doing good, for in due time we will reap if we do not grow weary."* It is discouraging to continue to do right and receive no word of thanks or see no tangible results. But Paul challenged the Galatians as he challenges us to keep on doing good and to trust God for the results. In due time, we will reap a harvest of blessing.

A **TRIUMPHANT OVERCOMER**:
1. Refuses to grow weary.
2. Keeps on doing good.
3. Recognizes their due season is coming.
4. Is committed to reaping.
5. Does not lose heart.

What specific challenge are you facing today? If you look at this situation through the characteristics of a **TRIUMPHANT OVERCOMER**, how would it change the way you see things?

A **TRIUMPHANT OVERCOMER'S** perspective is from the top of the "mountain" instead of the bottom. When you understand that the Greater One lives in you and gives you the power to overcome and live triumphantly, you change your standpoint. Below you will find the eight rewards of overcoming found in Revelation.

1. Revelation 2:7 to the Church at Ephesus – *"He who has an ear, let Him hear what the Spirit says to the churches. To him who overcomes, I will grant to eat of the tree of life which is in the Paradise of God."*

Are you a Triumphant Overcomer?

To overcome is to be victorious by believing in Christ, persevering, remaining faithful and living as one who follows Christ. Such a life brings hope and great rewards.

2. Revelation 2:11 to the Church at Smyrna - *"He who has an ear, let him hear what the Spirit says to the churches. He who overcomes will not be hurt by the second death."*

Pain is a part of life, but it is never easy to suffer, no matter what the cause. Jesus commended the church at Smyrna for its faith in suffering. He then encouraged the believers that they need not fear the future if they remained faithful. If you are experiencing difficult times, don't let them turn you away from God. Instead, let them draw you toward greater faithfulness. Trust God and remember your heavenly reward.

3. Revelation 2:17 to the Church at Pergamum - *"He who has an ear, let him hear what the Spirit says to the churches. To him who overcomes, to him, I will give some of the hidden manna, and I will give him a white stone, and a new name written on the stone which no one knows but he who receives it."*

The "Hidden manna" suggests the spiritual nourishment that the faithful believers will receive. As the Israelites traveled toward the promised land, God provided manna from heaven for their physical nourishment. Jesus, as the Bread of Life, provides spiritual nourishment that satisfies our deepest hunger.

It is unclear what the white stones are or exactly what the names on each will be but because they relate to the hidden manna, they may be symbols of the believer's eternal nourishment or eternal life.

The stones are significant because each will bear the new name of every person who truly believes in Christ. They are the evidence that a person has overcome and been accepted by God and declared worthy to receive eternal life. A person's name represented his or her character. God will give us new names and new hearts.

4. Revelation 2:26-28 to the Church at Thyatira – *"He who overcomes, and he who keeps My deeds until the end, to him I will give authority over the nations; and he shall rule them with a rod of iron, as the vessels of the potter are broken*

to pieces, as I also have received authority from My Father; and I will give him the morning star."

We should hold tightly to the basics of our Christian faith and view with caution and counsel any new teaching that turns us away from the Bible, the fellowship of our church, or our basic confession of faith. Christ says that those who overcome (those who remain faithful until the end and continue to please God) will rule over Christ's enemies and reign with Him as He judges evil.

5. Revelation 3:5 to the church at Sardis – *"He who overcomes will thus be clothed in white garments, and I will not erase his name from the book of life, and I will confess his name before My Father and before His angels."*

To be "clothed in white garments" means to be set apart for God and made pure. Christ promises future honor and eternal life to those who stand firm in their faith. The names of all believers are registered in the book of life. This book symbolizes God's knowledge of who belongs to Him. All such people are guaranteed a listing in the book of life and are introduced to the hosts of heaven as belonging to Christ.

6. Revelation 3:12 to the church at Philadelphia - *"He who overcomes, I will make him a pillar in the temple of My God, and he will not go out from it anymore; and I will write on him the name of My God, and the name of the city of My God, the new Jerusalem, which comes down out of heaven from My God, and My new name."*

The new Jerusalem is the future dwelling of the people of God. We will have a new citizenship in God's future kingdom. Everything will be new, pure and secure.

7. Revelation 3:21 to the church at Laodicea – *"He who overcomes, I will grant to him to sit down with Me on My throne, as I also overcame and sat down with My Father on His throne."*

God is faithful to His children, and although we may suffer great hardships here, God promises that someday we will live eternally with Him.

8. Revelation 21:7-8 to all overcomers – *"He who overcomes will inherit these things, and I will be his God and he will be My son. But for the cowardly and unbelieving and abominable and murderers and immoral persons and*

Are you a Triumphant Overcomer?

sorcerers and idolaters and all liars, their part will be in the lake that burns with fire and brimstone, which is the second death."

The "cowardly" are not those who are fainthearted in their faith or who sometimes doubt or question, but those who turn back from following God. They are not brave enough to stand up for Christ; they are not humble enough to accept His authority over their lives. They are put on the same list as the unbelieving, the vile, the murderers, the liars, the idolaters, the sexually immoral and the practicing of magic arts.

People who overcome endure "to the end." They will receive the rewards that God promised: (1) eating from the tree of life, (2) escaping the lake of fire, (3) receiving a special name, (4) having authority over the nations, (5) being included in the book of life, (6) being a pillar in God's spiritual temple, (7) sitting with Christ on His throne and (8) a heavenly inheritance. Those who can endure the testing of evil, remain faithful and overcome will be rewarded by God.

So again, I ask, are you living like a **TRIUMPHANT OVERCOMER**? Do you feel like a **TRIUMPHANT OVERCOMER**?

LaKesha L. Williams

"Come on over" whatever you're facing today, start living life victoriously in Christ and wait with great anticipation to reap the rewards of overcoming triumphantly, that is our hope!

Are you a Triumphant Overcomer?

A TRIUMPHANT OVERCOMERS PRAYER

As you just read, the book of Revelation has incredible promises that are associated with overcomers. This prayer condenses all of these promises into one place to allow you to lay hold of all that God has set aside for His overcomers!

Father, I come before you in prayer in the mighty name of Jesus. My declaration is that I choose to be an overcomer in Christ. I surrender myself to the journey you have set aside for me and I choose to press into the mark of the prize which is the high calling in Jesus Christ. I declare that as a result of my life and response to your commands it will be said to me, "Well done, thou good and faithful servant". I choose to partake of the promises associated with being an overcomer and I speak them over my life.

Along with the overcomers from the church of Ephesus, it will be given to me to eat of the tree of life, which is in the paradise of God.

Along with the overcomers from the church of Smyrna, I will not be hurt by the second death.

Along with the overcomers from the church of Pergamos, it will be given to me to eat of the hidden manna. I receive a white a stone and on the stone a new name which no one knows but the one who receives it.

Along with the overcomers from the church of Thyatira, I will be given power over the nations. With Jesus, I will rule them with a rod of iron, they shall be dashed to pieces like a potter's vessel. I also receive the morning star.

Along with the overcomers from the church of Sardis, I will retain garments that are not defiled. I will walk worthy with you Lord, in white garments. My name will not be blotted out of the book of Life and You, Lord Jesus, will confess my name before the Father and His angels.

Along with the overcomers from the church of Philadelphia, I will be made a pillar in the temple of God and shall go out no more. Upon me will be written the name of My God, the name of the city of My God, the New Jerusalem, which comes down from heaven from My God. Upon me Jesus will also write His new name.

Along with the overcomers from the church of Laodicea, it will be granted to me to sit with Jesus upon His throne, as He overcame and sat down with the Father upon His throne.

I decree these promises over my life in the mighty name of Jesus Christ. Amen.

Prayer Credit: Daniel Duval
https://www.bridemovement.com/over-comer-prayer/)

ABOUT THE VISIONARY AUTHOR

LaKesha L. Williams, acclaimed author, speaker and minister of the Gospel of Jesus Christ, was born to parents Doris & Cleo Williams in Raleigh, North Carolina in 1983. To know LaKesha is to experience a calming spirit infused with gut-wrenching laughter at unexpected times. She has a passion for giving, which is demonstrated wholeheartedly through her founding of Born Overcomers Inc. a need based nonprofit organization & movement dedicated to promoting the belief that we were all Born to Overcome.

She has authored ten books; including three bestsellers; and is also a featured co-author in Open Your G.I.F.T.S. presented by actress & comedian Kim Coles. She is also the Owner and Lead Visionary of The Vision to Fruition Group LLC, a consulting firm dedicated to helping others bring their visions to fruition. In 2015, LaKesha received the Sista's Inspiring Sista's Phenomenal Woman Award, since she has gone on to become the 2016 Indie Author Legacy Award Recipient in the Author on the Rise category, a 2016 Metro Phenomenal Woman Honoree, a 2017 TDK Publishing Author of the Year nominee & the 2018 iShine Awards winner for Author of the Year. LaKesha is currently a student at Capital Bible Seminary and Graduate School pursuing a dual Master's in Christian Care and Divinity.

LaKesha, as a virgin herself, is also an advocate of abstinence, purity & virginity until marriage. Currently, LaKesha resides in Maryland & enjoys serving in the community, fellowshipping with her church family at The Remnant of Hope International Church in Prince Frederick Maryland under the leadership of Pastor Margo Gross and spending time with her family & friends watching movies, sharing stories & creating new memories.

Contact

Phone: 240-343-3563

Email: info@lakeshalwilliams.com

Web: www.vision-fruition.com

Facebook Pages:

Born Overcomers Inc.

The Vision to Fruition Group

Coach Kesha, Visionary Overcomer

Personal Facebook:

www.facebook.com/lakesha.williams

Twitter: @mslakeshaw

Instagram: @lakeshalwilliams

ABOUT THE PUBLISHER

At The Vision to Fruition Publishing House, we are dedicated to helping others bring their personal, business, ministry & nonprofit visions to fruition.

If you want to write a book, The Vision to Fruition Publishing House will help you walk through the process and set you up for success! At The Vision to Fruition Group we don't have clients, we have Visionaries. We provide solutions to equip others to pursue their visions & dreams with reckless abandon.

We have published more than twenty-five authors, several of which were #1 Amazon Bestsellers. We would love for you to join our family of Visionaries as well!

Learn more here: www.vision-fruition.com

www.ingramcontent.com/pod-product-compliance
Lightning Source LLC
Chambersburg PA
CBHW070918160426
43193CB00011B/1512